LOST
JEFFERSON
CITY

LOST
JEFFERSON CITY

MICHELLE BROOKS

THE
History
PRESS

Published by The History Press
Charleston, SC
www.historypress.com

First published 2022

Manufactured in the United States

ISBN 9781467150354

Library of Congress Control Number: 2021950606

This book is dedicated to my mother, Melinda Susannah, who passed away during its preparation. She was my biggest fan, always holding higher hopes for me.

CONTENTS

CONTENTS

PREFACE

D uring my nearly twenty years as a reporter with the *Jefferson City News Tribune*, part of my coverage responsibilities included historic preservation.

I was introduced to the passionate promoters of this idea in the Capital City during the removals of the Cook Mansion on West Main Street, in what became the Lower Jefferson Conservation District, and the Lohman House, which once overlooked the city from Jefferson Street and is now the Salvation Army.

Gregory Stockard spent several conversations with me explaining the value of the architectural landscape to reflect the city's past.

In the early 2000s, a handful of people were renovating historic homes. During the last two decades, the local sentiment has shifted to support such endeavors. Slowly, city government is coming on board, too.

This book, *Lost Jefferson City*, is a remembrance of places that once held great community value or architectural interest and are now gone. Perhaps it will inspire future property owners to preserve the historic cityscape while providing modern-day living or business services.

ACKNOWLEDGEMENTS

From the first idea of this book, collaboration was a top priority.

Thank you to Jenny Smith and Deborah Goldammer, veteran researchers of local history, particularly historic properties. The bulk of the research for the "Lost Homes" section was provided by these generous and committed ladies.

To Janet Maurer, Patsy Johnson and Lucia Kincheloe, thank you for sharing the in-depth research and development put into creating the information panels to be installed along the Jefferson City Greenway through the former Foot area.

Travis Crede has devoted years to collecting clippings, photos and other bits and pieces of the nearly 150-year-old baseball tradition in Jefferson City. Hopefully, he will compile a book of his findings.

The author is grateful to Nancy Arnold Thompson for her personal support, as well as her information about local cemeteries.

Others who helped provide clarification and greater understanding include Don and Joyce Webb, Tim Young, Walter Schroeder, Ruthie Caplinger, Gail Severance, Patti Schmutzler, Jackie Trippensee, Jeremy Amick, Amy VanOverschelde, Laura Reed, Katherine Owens and Pat Kliethermes.

For help gathering photos, thank you to the Lincoln University Archive, Stephen Brooks, Darrell Strope, Joyce Logan Webb, Janet Maurer, Nancy Thompson and the Missouri State Archives.

The author is forever grateful for local newspapers, oral histories preserved by the Missouri State Museum and the Historic City of Jefferson and repositories like the Missouri State Archives and the State Historic Society of Missouri.

INTRODUCTION

Consider this book a sampler of the many places and properties that were once part of the physical fabric of Jefferson City.

For example, the Foot, an integral place in the twentieth-century African American community, requires its own book to cover the internal intricacies and external politics of the time.

The Mill Bottom also has more life and locales than were addressed here.

But it would have been impossible to write a book about "Lost Jefferson City" without highlighting these once-vital districts.

The other sections of this book were selected for their interest and variety, not necessarily for their historic priority.

I hope that readers will close this book with a greater appreciation for the city's past and the growth that brought us into the twenty-first century.

PART I

THE MILL BOTTOM

Chapter 1

ORIGINS

W hen the first two hundred lots in Jefferson City were auctioned in May 1823, the flat land on the riverfront immediately west of the planned capitol hill was popular property.

William Jones, who had operated a tavern on the site before Missouri even was accepted into the Union, bought the western corner lot of Water and Harrison Streets, just north of today's Secretary of State building. Soon after, Jefferson T. Rogers set up Rogers Landing for ferry service at the north end of Harrison Street, which crossed north to the Callaway County side.

McDaniel Dorris bought the western corner lot of Water Street and Broadway, where he operated the first distillery near a spring.[1]

Land speculators, including Peter Bass, John Brown, James Moss and Anson Bennett, also laid claim to choice corner lots in the second neighborhood in Jefferson City, following uptown.

This area was first called the Goose Bottom because "a large number of geese were raised on the bottom and swam [Weir's] Creek."[2]

The General Assembly met in the newly built statehouse east of the future capitol hill in 1826. A handful of buildings had been erected in town by then, mostly around the 100 block of Madison and Jefferson Streets, where the government met and the main boat landing was located.

Ten years later, the "best corner lots [were] still encumbered with native crab tree and principal streets thickly shaded with hazel." However, Main Street, which was the western access to the city, had been improved with bridges over Weir's Creek and elsewhere.[3] At one time, a half-dozen artistic cement bridges crossed the creek, including the five-hundred-foot-long viaduct extending High Street over what became Missouri Boulevard.[4]

By 1839, the first permanent capitol was nearly complete on the central hilltop, and Jefferson City was organized as a city. While most of the early land speculators were of southern heritage, the men and families who developed the Goose Bottom, making it the Mill Bottom, were primarily German-speaking immigrants.

In those earliest years, a bridge crossed what was called Big Creek before becoming Weir's Creek. The first building west of that bridge was owned by Widow Rains, below the sign "private entertainment."[5]

Christopher Kolkmeyer, one of the city's earliest German immigrants, arrived in 1836. According to author James E. Ford, at one time Kolkmeyer's was the only house in the Goose Bottom.[6] He and his brother, Frederick, owned a quarry, about where the Missouri Secretary of State's office is today, which supported their road and gutter business.

In addition to the early Jones' tavern, Rogers Landing and Kolkmeyer quarry, Captain Jefferson Rogers also opened a tanyard in the area, and Mathias Wallendorf was operating a sawmill, built by W.P. Riggins, on Water Street by 1847.[7]

Pacific Railroad began land speculating after it was granted $2 million by the Missouri General Assembly in 1851.[8] That included Jefferson City and the Mill Bottom, particularly.[9]

Then, G.H. Dulle and his German-speaking partners built the first mill at the southeast corner of Walnut and Main Streets, setting the Goose Bottom on a new course for growth.

By the Civil War, Stephen Bergman was operating a grocery and drugstore in the 600 block of West Main, and several homes had been built in the German vernacular style, of which only a few examples remain today.

During the Civil War, the Union Fort College Hill occupied land west of the Mill Bottom, with soldiers camped to the corner of West Main and Harrison Streets.[10]

Soon after the war, the 300 to 700 blocks of West Main were filling with merchants and residences. West of the capitol, John Fitzpatrick operated a blacksmith and wagon-making shop. Henry Karges built cabinets at his home, and Mrs. Henry Rephlo kept a grocery store. Dr. A. Peabody set up a practice, and Mathias Wallendorf's sawmill was doing good business. The ferry at Harrison Street was under Jones & Maus, and Dulle added a brickyard to his milling operation. Carpenter Anton Moeller opened a lumberyard, and other general stores were set up by Jacque Jacquet, Mary Ann Moller, G. Droste and Lorenz Franz.

Pencil sketch by Edward Roby of 1859 Jefferson City, looking east from above Bolivar Street. *Photo courtesy of Missouri State Archives, Summers Collection.*

Homes were scattered among the hills, the streets were rough and unpaved and the walks were lighted with coal oil lamps.[11] But anchored by the Franz & Brother brewery on Bolivar Street and the St. Peter Catholic Church on Broadway, the Mill Bottom soon became a self-supporting, working-class neighborhood.[12]

Although primarily German-speaking Catholics, the Mill Bottom residents and proprietors were involved in their greater community. For example, they joined with German-speaking Protestants for projects, such as the "German Fair for the benefit of orphans of the German soldiers who have fallen during the present war" with France in October 1870.[13] And by the Civil War, Dr. Bernard Bruns had become the town's first German-speaking mayor.

One major influence the German-speaking immigrants had on the city's development was creating a "town of brick."[14] At its peak, the Mill Bottom was lined with brick buildings, and the town at large had passed an ordinance requiring brick construction.

"In many respects the Mill Bottom was as important in the development of Jefferson City as the higher elevation commercial zone to the southeast," wrote Craig Sturdevant and Gary Kremer in *Jefferson City Historic District Capitol West.*[15]

Chapter 2

MAKING DRINKS

The oldest profession and the earliest residents in what became the Mill Bottom were tied to alcohol. The type of consumable may have changed over the next 150 years, but the drink and its social function remained constant—even through Prohibition.

William Jones was one of two men living in the area when it was designated the permanent seat of government. A Revolutionary War veteran, Jones set up a tavern before 1819 on the river's edge near a spring, where Rogers Landing developed at the north end of Harrison Street.

After Cole County was created, Jones received a license to keep a ferry in the township of Jefferson in 1822. He served as justice of the peace in 1824 and was an original city trustee when Jefferson City incorporated in 1825.[16] When official lots were measured and auctioned in May 1823, he officially bought the land for his tavern.[17] Jones' son, Robert, took over the tavern business about 1829, when William Jones moved to Rocheport.[18]

Ferry captain Jefferson T. Rogers bought the lot and ferry landing, where he built a magnificent stone home in 1840 that stood until the railroad acquired the property at the turn of the twentieth century.

Before the legislature arrived for the first time in 1826, Irishman McDaniel Dorris had set up a distillery between Jones' tavern and the future capitol site. About 1859, he moved his home and operation to the east end of town, at the corner of McCarty and Lafayette Streets.[19] Dorris later operated a saloon at 304 Madison Street, where his whiskey, peach brandy and applejack were kept.[20]

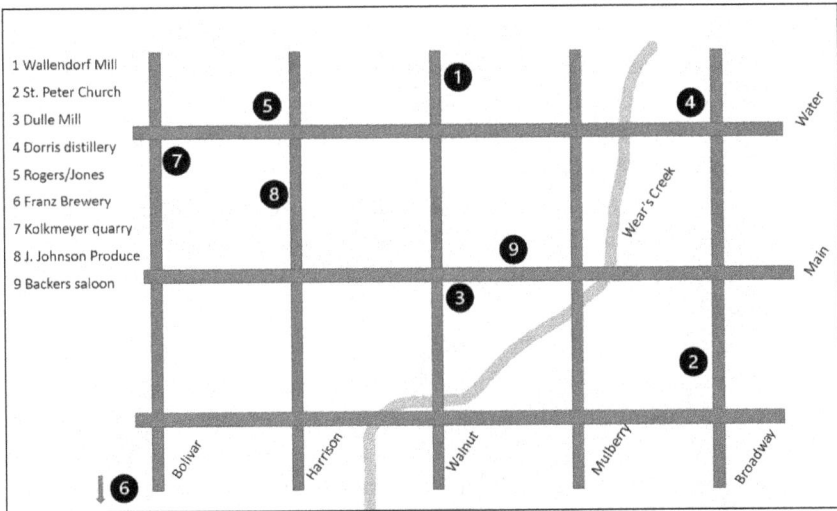

1 Wallendorf Mill
2 St. Peter Church
3 Dulle Mill
4 Dorris distillery
5 Rogers/Jones
6 Franz Brewery
7 Kolkmeyer quarry
8 J. Johnson Produce
9 Backers saloon

Map of early alcohol production and sales in the Mill Bottom. *Map by Michelle and Stephen Brooks.*

Dr. Robert Young recalled Dorris' spirits were "clear as spring water." And despite Dorris' claims that "his whiskey was as innocent as the same quantity of buttermilk," someone else claimed that "if a man got drunk on it, it took a week to get sober again."[21]

In the early days, liquor was not taxed, so Dorris could make and sell any amount.[22] The son of a Baptist pioneer minister, Dorris was an honored, forty-year member of the Masons. His obituary said he outlived everyone living in the city in 1825, with the exception of Hiram Baber.[23]

Doris was remembered for having a "most happy disposition, always rendering him contented with himself and the world and thus, no doubt, greatly contributing to prolonged life....He was distinguished for an uprightness and honesty, which never suffered the slightest taint of blemish."[24]

As German-speaking immigrants arrived, they brought their taste for beer, which at first had to be home brewed, according to Old Munichburg historian Walter Schroeder.[25] The first-known beer house, Jefferson City Brewery, was opened in 1844 by Charles Gesser at the corner of Main and Washington Streets, "opposite the Capitol."[26]

Then, in 1847, John C. Gundelfinger opened the Missouri Brewery in the 100 block of West Dunklin.[27] Its popularity benefited from the German-speaking Union troops stationed in Jefferson City, who did not drink whiskey.[28] By 1868, Gundelfinger's was the "largest brewery west of St. Louis." The

Wagner Brewery, which had operated twenty-eight years in Schubert, relocated to Jefferson City in 1870, when it bought Gundelfinger's business, changing the name from City Brewery to George Wagner Brewery.[29]

The Mill Bottom had its own brewery, which the Franz brothers built on the hill near G.H. Dulle's home.

Lorenz and Andreas Franz arrived in Jefferson City in 1865, buying the 173-acre farm of Peter McLain.[30] They were born in Bavaria, immigrating first to Pittsburg, Pennsylvania, and then Mt. Carroll, Illinois, where they were tailors.[31]

They began brewing locally in 1867.[32]

In 1869, after a two-year partnership with Joseph Geissler, they dissolved Geissler & Company and formed Franz & Brother, averaging 150 barrels per month by 1873.[33] However, George Wagner was generating twice that in his brewery on Dunklin Street, which was on its way to becoming one of the largest breweries in the state.[34] "Breweries of Jefferson City do a much larger business than people generally suppose," a local newspaper said.[35]

In 1874, the brothers opened the Franz Brothers Brewery at the intersection of Miller and Bolivar Streets. It was Jefferson City's fourth brewery, and the brothers operated it for eighteen years.[36]

They competed with the Southside C&L Wagner Brewery, owned by the sons of Paulus Wagner, which was bought by Jacob F. Moerschel in 1892.[37] A note from the World's Exposition in Philadelphia, Pennsylvania, in 1876 observed, "Local patriots will insist that Wagner's and Franz's beer is a far superior beverage to the thin, insipid stuff made by Philadelphia brewers."[38]

The Franz Brothers Brewery closed in 1891, the result of a city council ordinance—opposed by then-alderman Lorenz Franz—increasing the saloon license from $150 to $500 per year.[39]

The Moerschel family bought the Franz property, including four half-acre lots and a fine artesian well, in 1895, and then donated it to the Sisters of St. Mary for the original St. Mary's Hospital (1904–2014).[40]

The Franz brothers lived in the Mill Bottom area, also operating a mercantile there, and were active in St. Peter Church and the broader community.

Andreas Franz was a member of the 1883 church building committee; among the incorporators of the St. Peter's Catholic Cemetery Association in 1884; and an organizer of the St. Peter Benevolent Society in 1866, serving as president from 1879 to 1884.[41]

Lorenz Franz served the Mill Bottom area as a city alderman and was active in neighborhood politics. He also was president of the Catholic Knights of America #214.[42]

Like other breweries that came and went—including Gundelfinger, Turner and Friemel—the Franz brewery property provided a beer garden, popular for community picnics or Sunday afternoon relaxation. It became the preferred location for Mill Bottom residents and St. Peter Church functions.

For example, when the St. Peter Benevolent Society celebrated its twenty-fifth anniversary in 1891, it held a procession from the church to Franz Garden, where the Jefferson City Silver Cornet Band and Professor Friemel's string band were engaged to play for the afternoon.[43]

The Franz Garden "was advertised as 'high and airy with a magnificent view and friendly service…the most beautiful pleasure spot in the region. The best drinks, cigars, etc., always on hand; care will be taken to maintain strict order.' It was a 'pleasant and shady resort, supplied with dancing floor, beer stands, etc.'"[44]

The site included the Franz residence, a saloon and an icehouse, in addition to the beer garden and brewery complex, all surrounded by the European-style stone retaining walls, fifty feet above Weir's Creek. The brewery sat about where the remaining parking garage of the old St. Mary's Hospital now sits on Bolivar Street. The Franz beer was advertised as a "tasty, unadulterated and nourishing" lager.

The St. Louis–based William J. Lemp Brewery established a presence in Jefferson City in 1892, buying Captain Rogers' mansion at Water and Harrison Streets near the ferry landing.[45] Lemp converted the mansion into a storage facility, Jacob Schmidt became the local agent and Nicholas Schmidt drove the Lemp beer wagon.

Jacob Schmidt, who emigrated from Saarland at age sixteen, kept kegs and bottles on hand for trade.[46] A musician, he also kept a violin and hand organ handy in his saloons.[47]

Schmidt had a farm on the Moreau River, where he carved river ice to sell in the city. As operator of the Farmers Home hotel and saloon in Old Munichburg, in the 1880s, Schmidt was known as the "Moreau Eisbär" or the "Moreau Polar Bear," according to author Walter Schroeder.[48]

Without artificial refrigeration, ice was a necessity for this industry. In the winter, blocks of ice from the rivers or creeks would be cut and stored underneath thick layers of straw to last through the summer heat.[49]

Saloons became more prevalent after the Civil War. "By the 1890s saloons were accessible within a few blocks to almost anyone in Jefferson City. The proprietor of virtually every saloon was a man of German birth or parentage," Schroeder writes in his book *Breweries and Saloons*.[50]

For example, Gerard "Henry" Backers emigrated with his family from Hanover to Elston when he was nine, in 1860. He began working for the G.H. Dulle Milling Company in 1882, and by 1897 he was operating a saloon at his residence at 411 West Main Street. He had moved his saloon, and his sand dealership, to 416 West Main Street by 1900 and to 420 West Main Street by 1904. By 1908, he had dropped the saloon and was living at 312 West Main Street.

Lemp's Beer Depot relocated to the 400 block of West Main Street about 1908. Schmidt, who also lived in the Mill Bottom, returned to restaurant and boardinghouse operations at 416 West Main Street, until his death in 1914 of cirrhosis of the liver at age eighty-one.[51]

By 1917, St. Louis' Anheuser Busch Company had moved into the Mill Bottom with a location at 428 West Main Street.

Jefferson City Bottling Works, under F.E. Jones, had opened about 1906 at 509 West Main Street. When Prohibition knocked out the liquor trade, several businesses converted to soft drinks. The Moerschels, unable to produce their successful beer, converted to soda, including the Coca-Cola franchise in 1922. Several saloons also converted their services to soda parlors.

When Prohibition was lifted, Jefferson City's Central Labor Union organized a parade with local musicians through the business district. And eight local distributors were ready the morning of April 7, 1933, to receive carloads of beer from St. Louis and trucks from St. Joseph.[52]

"Restaurants and fountains where lunches are served [will] handle the amber fluid," one newspaper reported in advance of the anticipated repeal.[53]

After World War II, franchise beers took hold, especially when, in 1947, the only local brewer, Capitol Brewery, managed by Ernst Moerschel, closed its South Side operation.[54] More bars opened along West Main Street and the surrounding blocks, including Friel's Tavern and Nite After Nite, Blue Goose, Step Inn, Club Bar, Eddie's Tap Room and Goodin's Tap Room.[55]

The Mill Bottom continued to be the location for storage and distributorships for decades. They included Ramsey Supply for Budweiser and Alpen Brau; Ben Fechtel for EMS and Stag; Jefferson City Bottling Company for Goetz Country Club out of St. Joseph; Nehi Bottling Company for Falstaff of St. Louis; and Jefferson City Produce Company for Schlitz from Milwaukee, Wisconsin.[56]

The J. Johnson Fruit and Produce Company was the post-Prohibition distributor for Griesedieck Brothers Beer until 1957, when Falstaff bought and closed its competitor. The J. Johnson Produce Company was located at 110 Harrison Street in a two-story blonde brick building near the river.

The J. Johnson Produce Company was a longtime business in the Mill Bottom. *Photo courtesy of Don Whitener.*

Clyde Whitener had joined the wholesale grocery dealer in 1936. Its canvas-covered delivery trucks drove to St. Louis at least twice a week for fresh product and then around the immediate Jefferson City area to deliver to the dozens of neighborhood stores.[57]

By 1940, Ben Fechtel had opened Fechtel Beverage Company at 424 West Main Street, and by 1957, it was distributor for Stag, Schlitz and Lemp beer, Dad's root beer and other sodas.[58] With the loss of the Griesedieck contract, Whitener worked for Fechtel's distributorship about ten years, until he bought out Paul Schmidt for the Falstaff distributorship.

When urban renewal was claiming the last vestiges of the Mill Bottom's former glory, Whitener's Falstaff and Miller business was relocated to 607 Dix Road, where Mark's Mobile Glass is today.[59] It was the last of the distributorships to leave the Mill Bottom.

Chapter 3

NAMESAKE

The first mill in the Goose Bottom—which would be remembered for its namesake as the "Mill Bottom"—was introduced by the partnership of Bernard Bruns, Gerhard Dulle and John H. Kroeger in 1854. Capital Mills, a small, two-story grain mill, was erected at the southeast corner of Walnut and West Main Streets.

These three German-speaking immigrants and members of St. Peter Church also lived near the area they designated for their new business venture.

Kroeger was a blacksmith and Bruns a doctor and entrepreneur.

When Gerhard Dulle arrived as a teenager, he already had "fixed habits of industry and frugality," first working as a hod carrier and then starting his first business to provide wood to the Missouri State Penitentiary.[60] He expanded into the dairy business and then bought the former Mitchell's Mill, opened in 1846 on Jefferson Street.[61]

Harden Casey, one of the first twenty-six residents of Jefferson City, is credited with opening the first horse-powered grinding mill in the city after buying the northeast corner lot at High and Madison Streets in 1825.[62] Robert A. Ewing opened a second mill on the south edge of town, before Mitchell opened his first steam-powered mill in 1844 on the east side of the 100 block of Jefferson Street.[63]

Because the process was slow, the Mitchell mill only supplied local customers with grinding their corn or wheat.[64] When the trio started the Goose Bottom mill, it opened possibilities for broader commerce.

Bruns traveled in 1832 from Westphalia to St. Louis, where he met adventurer-author Nicholas Hesse. The pair traveled to Osage City, where the former bought land and contracted for a house to be built. Dr. Bruns, a graduate of Bonn University, returned home for his family, whom he brought with a small colony of their neighbors to settle Westphalia, Missouri.[65]

The Bruns family moved to Jefferson City in 1853, opening a boardinghouse on the south side of the 100 block of West High Street. The same year the Goose Bottom mill went up, in 1854, Bruns bought the brick building, known today as the Hope Building, at the same spot where Harden Casey had erected the town's first mill.[66]

For a decade, Bruns ran a mercantile and his medical practice from the main floor, and the family lived on the second floor.[67] Soon after the Civil War began in June 1861, Dr. Bruns was appointed lieutenant-surgeon of the First Regiment Home Guards.[68]

Bruns died in 1864, while serving as the city's mayor.[69] Then Kroeger died in 1865.[70]

Dulle took on a new partner, Heinrich Herman Altgilbers, another German-speaking member of St. Peter, as well as laborer G.H. Kroeger.[71]

Altgilbers was a brickmaker from Westphalia who had relocated to Jefferson City by 1860.[72] He emigrated from Dahlem in 1846, to St. Louis and then Ohio.[73] He was a charter member and the first treasurer of the St. Peter Benevolent Society in 1866, and he served as president twice.[74]

Altgilbers owned a resort southwest of town on St. Mary's Boulevard, which was used for the benevolent society's annual picnics, as well as Fourth of July gatherings for more than a decade.[75] "This celebration is always looked forward to with much pleasure. It is a picnic on a grand scale," the *People's Tribune* said in 1871 of the society's anniversary.[76]

By 1870, Dulle's oldest son, Henry, and stepson, J.W. Schulte, had joined him in the mill business.[77] At this time, the two-story, pre–Civil War mill was replaced with a four-story mill, called Capital Star Mills, which had a capacity of three hundred barrels of flour per day.[78]

In 1873, the Altgilbers-Dulle-Kroeger partnership dissolved with the retirement of Dulle, but the business retained the G.H. Dulle name.[79]

The new business, under the sons, built Victoria Mill in 1876 at 320 West Main Street, which was rebuilt in 1882 after a fire.[80] By 1878, Custom Mills was operated by G.H. Dulle & Company and the Merchant Mill by G.H. Dulle & Sons.[81]

The Dulle firm saw its first competition in 1877 from fellow Mill Bottom entrepreneur Mathias Wallendorf. He replaced his sawmill, on the river

The Victoria Mill, built by the G.H. Dulle Milling Company, was among the businesses that gave the West Main Street neighborhood its name. *Photo courtesy of Cole County Historical Society.*

and near the railroad tracks, with the Pacific Mill at 401 Water Street with proprietors Wallendorf, Blume and Huegel.[82]

Wallendorf & Company operated Pacific Mills for at least a year, competing with Dulle's Custom Mill and Merchant Mill.[83] By 1881, Pacific Mills and Grain Dealer was operated by G. Charles Volkert, and it was vacant by 1885.[84]

Mathias Wallendorf was the first of his family to be naturalized in 1846. He was eighteen when his family of eight left Prussia in 1836, and he learned his carpentry skills from his father, Josephi. The Wallendorf family first settled south of town, building a double-dogtrot cabin—now the focal point of the Missouri Farm Bureau's museum.[85]

In 1840, the younger Wallendorf built a privy for the General Assembly and in 1871 constructed a fence around the capitol grounds.[86]

Before 1862, Wallendorf opened a sawmill on Mulberry Street at the railroad tracks. Supplied with "superior" wood from the area, the sawmill had a steady business, including businesses like the Henry & Preston—later Preston & Scovern—Saddle Tree Manufacturers, the largest of its kind in the nation at the time.[87]

The Pacific Mill's five-story brick building was repurposed in 1893 to manufacture excelsior, the fine wood product used for packing. The Henry Excelsior Company was managed by G.E. Lohman, later cashier of Merchant's Bank, with Lawrence Wagner as president and Fritz Truetzel as vice president.[88]

The ground floor was the engine and boiler room and baling department, and the second floor manufactured all grades of excelsior.[89] It had twelve machines turning out sixty bales of excelsior each day at one hundred pounds each. The excelsior was sent by chute from the second to the first floors, where it was baled and carried by elevator to the third and fourth stories for storage. The bales could then be loaded directly onto train cars.

Dr. Joseph P. Porth was president of the Excelsior Manufacturing Company, renamed Pacific, which had relocated to 515 West Main Street in 1904 and lasted until about 1912.

Porth was the son of William Porth, one of the "most successful Mill Bottom Prussians."[90] William Porth's home at the southeast corner of Main and Bolivar Streets is one of the few remaining pieces of the earliest Mill Bottom. The cotton-rock structure was built by 1840, serving as one of the earliest general stores for the west end.

Dr. Porth, who graduated from St. Louis University and studied in Berlin, Paris, Vienna and Greifswald, operated his medical practice at street level from 1888 to 1923. The younger Porth was mayor in 1903, then served three terms as state representative.

In addition to continuing the excelsior-manufacturing plant, Porth oversaw property in Claremore, Oklahoma, owned by Jefferson Citians as the Missouri Central Oil and Gas Company. He was active in the St. Peter Benevolent Society and the Cole County Medical Association. He was among those who incorporated the Jefferson City Sanitarium.

Gerhard Dulle died in 1884, after serving as sheriff in 1866 and county collector from 1878 to 1882.

"A man of pleasing address and kindly nature, he made friends on every hand and soon had a strong hold on the esteem and affection of the people of our then small city," his 1884 obituary said.[91]

Gerhard Dulle's son Henry incorporated the milling business on January 22, 1885, with himself as president and his brother Bernard as vice president. J.W. Schulte, their older stepbrother, was secretary-treasurer and business manager.[92]

By 1892, the G.H. Dulle Mill operation took up nearly half a block on the south side of the 400 block of West Main Street, and Victoria Mills was still in operation across the street.[93] The Dulle family business added a massive grain elevator, capable of holding fifty thousand bushels of wheat, in 1895.[94]

A significant fire took much of the Dulle assets in 1896. But they rebuilt with brick across most of the 400 block of West Main Street, converting the Victoria Mill at 320 West Main Street to a warehouse.[95] The offices were located at 425 West Main Street, with the mill at 429 and the elevator at 433.[96]

In the early part of the twentieth century, the Capital Star Roller Mill, 425–431 West Main Street, was generating flour packaged as Dulle's Patent, Capital Star, Baker's Delight and Schulte Patent.[97] It was operated daily by twenty skilled millers and assistants at the full capacity of five hundred barrels of flour per day.[98]

"For nearly half a century, the name Dulle has been familiarly associated with what is best in flour," the 1900 *Illustrated Sketch Book* said.[99]

By 1929, G.H. Dulle Milling Company had been in operation on the same spot for seventy-five years. The main mill was at 425 West Main Street, and the 430 building was used as a warehouse.[100]

The Missouri Farmers Association (MFA) Central Co-op took over the property by 1951.[101] Before it took over the Dulle site, the Farmers' Elevator was located at 410 Mulberry Street. J.H. Kaiser was in charge in 1900, and Alex Alford and Martin A. Jaeger operated it by 1904.[102]

Map of early production and retail in the Mill Bottom. *Map by Michelle and Stephen Brooks.*

Back in 1867, Gerhard H. Dulle also had opened a brickyard on the east side of the 200 block of Harrison Street. Bricks from this yard were donated for the third and present St. Peter Church. By 1881, Dulle had relinquished the brickyard.[103]

However, Herman Altgilbers and Bernard H. Pohl each had opened brickyards by 1877, both located near the intersection of Bolivar and West High Streets. In 1881, the Pohl brickyard relocated to the 600 block of West Main Street.

A Prussian immigrant, Pohl reared eighteen children one block west of his brickyard. His son Martin J. Pohl took over in 1904. About 1908, the Pohls added a cement-block factory to their operation in the 200 block of Harrison Street. Then, son Otto B. Pohl took over the family business by 1912.

"I suspect that many of the celebrated, historic buildings on High Street were built from bricks, from clay mined and kiln-baked on the bluff that stretched from the 600 block of West Main to beneath the High Street viaduct. Sanborn maps neatly trace the retreat of that bluff as more and more of it got removed over the years; its loess clay converted into brick," South Side historian Walter Schroeder said.[104]

In 1895, the quality of clay from Jefferson City made it one of the top ten sites for brick manufacturing. At that time, the Pohls had competition from not only the Jefferson City Brick Yard—opened before 1892 at 1003 West High Street and later moved to West Main Street—but also the John Doehla & Company plant, newly opened and producing pressed bricks.[105]

Chapter 4

PRODUCTION AND RETAIL

U nlike the Uptown and South Side areas, which were primarily retail, the Mill Bottom produced as well as sold items. Much of that can be attributed to its proximity to the railroad tracks.

For example, the Porth & Spannagel pork house moved from Syracuse in Morgan County to Jefferson City about 1874, first interested in using the old Pacific Railroad roundhouse, which was not being used at the time.[106]

Instead, they built a new pork house at the northwest corner of Water and Harrison Streets, at Roger's Landing.[107] "Almost all the pork fattened in this vicinity and for miles around, finds a market [and] is here slaughtered," the *State Journal* reported.[108] At the state pork packers' convention in the fall of 1875, Spannagel and representatives from LaGrange and St. Joseph were the only ones not from St. Louis.

The Jefferson City pork-packing business lasted only about a decade, when Prussian immigrant Edward Spannagel moved to St. Louis.

By 1885, a livestock pen had been built at the southeast corner of Water and Harrison Streets, with the barnyard office at 600 West Main Street.[109] The operation passed from John W. Gordon, to Sinclair & Sullens, to Sinclair & McMillain, and then John Sinclair had sole ownership.

Sinclair's parents emigrated from Ireland to Callaway County, and he had moved to Jefferson City by the age of thirty in 1888. He was the local stock dealer at 118 Harrison Street from at least 1894 to 1935. In partnership with the Jefferson City Chamber of Commerce, the Sinclair Stock Yard began holding community stock sales in 1934.[110]

Sinclair's 120-acre farm on the north side of Ten Mile Drive near Schumate Chapel was sold to the St. Peter Catholic Cemetery Association in 1934 for what is now Resurrection Cemetery.[111] Sinclair served as a longtime director of Exchange National Bank.[112]

A feed store—a necessity with a livestock barn nearby—opened at 120 Harrison Street about 1894. John Edward Wells operated it for many years, before Ed Ruwart and Oliver Bassman took over and renamed it the Jefferson City Produce Company.

Wells was born in Jefferson City to one of its prominent pioneer families and educated at Westminster College. He sold the land where both East Elementary and Immaculate Conception Schools now sit.[113]

By 1908, the Jefferson City Produce Company included warehousing, stock barns, a feed barn and a salt house, operated by Frank Long, a skilled bookkeeper who suffered a nervous breakdown.[114] Long left about 1908 to work for Missouri Pacific Railroad as a clerk, and then, by 1925, he was keeping the books for G.H. Dulle Milling.

Later, Long committed suicide by muriatic acid poisoning, as the result of gambling debt. He had worked in the railroad ticket office, in banks and lastly for the city, where he had access to cash, which he "borrowed" for his habit.[115]

Jefferson City Produce Company, also the local dealer for Purina Mills out of St. Louis, built a fireproof brick building at the northwest corner of Harrison and Main Streets in 1915. Immediately north was the John Sinclair Livestock Barn, on the southwest corner of Water and Harrison Streets, with a hay barn and poultry feed store in between.[116]

In 1933, the *Daily Capital News* called the company "the oldest buying house in the city," even taking trappers' furs and skins.[117]

By 1951, J. Johnson Fruit and Produce Company was operating out of 110 Harrison Street, with Trip's Feed and Produce around the corner at 626 West Main Street.

Unlike today, workers and employers lived near their places of employment.

If one were to walk along West Main Street at the turn of the twentieth century, one would likely smell smoke from the towering stacks above one, the grind of machinery and the odors of livestock. One would pass two-story brick houses and lean-to frame homes in between grocers, general stores, saloons, business offices and warehouses.

Another staple of the Mill Bottom products was sand. Henry Backers was operating a sand dealership out of his saloon at 416 West Main Street by 1900. Before his death in 1903, Perrin Kay and his sons, with partner William Wolf,

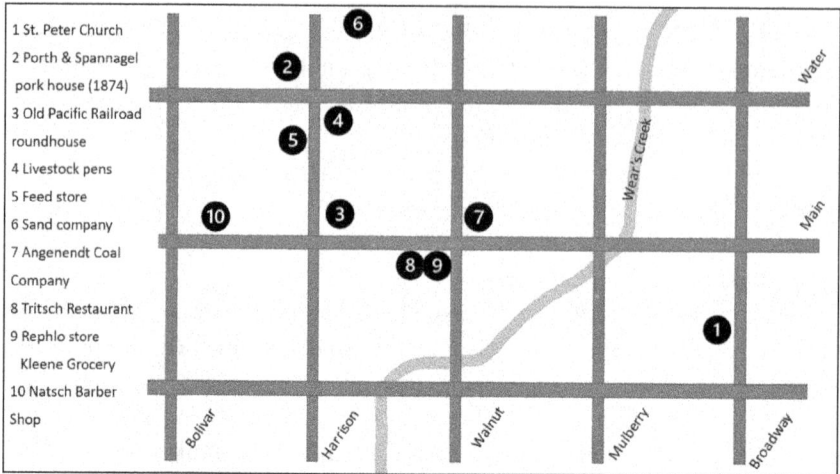

Map of early sales and production in the Mill Bottom. *Map by Michelle and Stephen Brooks.*

were dealing sand. The Kay brothers partnered with Henry J. Wallau in 1905 to form the Jefferson City Sand Company at 510 West Water Street.[118]

Captain Perrin Kay worked steamboats for forty-six years, including a Jefferson City expedition up the Yukon River to the Alaskan gold fields.[119] The Kay brothers were born on the Kansas edge of the Missouri River, entering river work at a young age.

The older brother, William Perrin Kay, was engineer at the sand company until he resumed work as a seaman.[120] Fred Ross Kay operated a steam shovel in Muskogee, Oklahoma, and then returned to steamboats along the Missouri River before becoming boiler inspector for the U.S. Bureau of Navigation and Steamboat Inspection.[121]

Henry J. Wallau retired from his distinguished construction career in 1912 to manage the sand business full time. He made his home in the Mill Bottom, just a few blocks away from the plant.

Emigrating from Alsbach in 1882, Wallau worked for local builder Fred Binder on the initial construction of the St. Peter Church. He opened his own shop in 1886, west of the Lohman Building on Water Street, and later operated the Capital City Planning Company south of his shop facing Main Street.[122]

His first major build was the Bockrath Shoe Store at 703 West Main Street in 1888, and his last was the original St. Mary's Hospital in 1904. Although those are both gone, his most memorable structure may be the 1898 Missouri Pacific Railroad station, which remains at the north end of

Monroe Street.[123] In the Mill Bottom area, he also built the 1889 section of today's St. Peter School and the G.H. Dulle Mill and grain elevator in 1895.

While Wallau's contributions as a builder are obvious, his involvement in his community, particularly the St. Peter Church parish, were equally significant. He served twice as mayor and seven times as alderman, focusing on road improvements such as the bridge over Weir's Creek at Miller Street.[124]

Wallau was the longest-serving president of the St. Peter Benevolent Society—twenty-two years. The organization held its members to high moral standards and supported their families in sickness or death.[125]

The city's businesses and government buildings closed during Wallau's funeral as a sign of respect. The society remembered him as a "man of high character, a real Christian in every way...untiring, self-sacrificing and courageous."[126]

The sand work was done by hand on a steep bank before steam and then electric machines became available.[127] Many a child had fun playing in the sand piles on the south side of the Missouri River, recalled South Side historian Walter Schroeder.

After Wallau's death in 1927, his sons, Al and George, took over the sand business and built the ninety-by-twenty-foot *J.H. Wallau* steamer, which pushed their barges for seventeen years.[128]

With proximity to the railroad tracks, the Mill Bottom became host to several coal companies, as well as the city's scales. Coal shops, like the Angenendt Coal Company, also known as the Consolidated Coal Company, opened as early as 1893. And with them came tinners, sheet metal work and furnace builders, like the J.W. Riner Company.

Theodore "Theo" Angenendt opened his wood and coal business in 1893 at the corner of Brooks and West Miller Streets. By 1912, he had moved it to the corner of Main and Mulberry Streets, where he employed six men and five wagons to haul the fuel off from the railroad deposits to customers.[129] By 1938, there were six coal dealers in the city.

Theo Angenendt emigrated from Dusseldorf at age twelve with his family, who settled on a farm near Stringtown before moving to Osage County. After serving with the Home Guards during the Civil War, he served as deputy sheriff and sheriff in Osage County. The family moved to Jefferson City in 1887, when he was involved in the addition construction of the second capitol. He was elected county presiding judge in 1908.[130]

At his death in 1924, his daughter Anna K. Norwood continued management.[131] Norwood was "one of the city's well-known businesswomen" when she died in 1941.[132]

She attended Mary's Home School, clerked at the Kaullen store in Mary's Home and then continued to live in Mary's Home after marrying Dr. John Norwood, a charter member of the Cole County Medical Association.[133]

A widow, Norwood and her three children moved to Jefferson City in 1901, when she took an active role in her father's coal business.[134] "She was very successful, increasing the business until it was one of the leading industries of its kind in Jefferson City."[135]

Norwood was a founding member of Immaculate Conception Church.[136] She was also politically active and owned considerable property in the city.[137]

Of course, the most substantial industry in the Mill Bottom would be the power plant in the 400 block of West Main Street, though the display room was uptown at 220 East High Street.

As automobiles emerged in the twentieth century, the Mill Bottom also became saturated with fuel stations and oil company product warehouses.

To support all of the working men and their families in the neighborhood, several retail stores, service providers and restaurants opened.

For example, the McKinney Brothers Café, now Sweet Smoke BBQ, started at 509 West Main Street as early as 1911. The location had been a bakery before that, and John G. Tritsch & Son Restaurant took the location in 1920.

John Tritsch was born in Indiana, where he worked in the saddle-tree industry. That brought him to Jefferson City in 1895 to work with the Sullivan Saddle Tree Company. Tritsch and his son, Robert, bought the café from the McKinney brothers in 1920, soon after the younger returned from military service in France with the 146th Field Artillery medical detachment.[138]

Three years later, John Tritsch was fatally shot during a holdup at the restaurant.[139] The shooter, William Gray, was freed twelve years later by Governor Guy Park and deported to England. John Tritsch had thought Gray was joking when he walked into his restaurant wearing a mask and said, "Stick 'em up."

Robert Tritsch continued to operate the restaurant until his death in 1950.

By 1900, the few blocks of West Main Street included three blacksmiths, a brick contractor and brick manufacturer, two dry goods stores, a harness and saddlery business, the mill, the livestock pens, a mattress manufacturer, a marble works, three poultry breeders, two saloons, a sand dealer, two wood and coal businesses, one tinware retailer, two shoe shops and a dressmaker.

Perhaps the longest-serving grocery location, before the Capital View Urban Renewal project, was at 501 West Main Street. Bernard Rephlo built a log general store in 1850 at the location, and his son Frank Rephlo replaced it with a substantial, two-story brick grocery and dry goods store in 1884.[140]

Joe Kleene Sr., about 1940, outside the Kleene Brothers Grocery, 501 West Main Street. *Photo courtesy of Missouri State Archives, Kleene Collection.*

Bernard and Helen (Nieters) Rephlo emigrated from Westphalia and Hanover, respectively, in 1837, stopping first in Jefferson City, where, as a stonemason, Bernard Rephlo helped build the second capitol. They moved to Taos, where he helped build the first log, second stone and third brick churches and then to Westphalia, where he helped build the stone church there.[141]

Bernard Rephlo died just eight years after moving to Jefferson City, and his wife, Helen, took charge of the business, helped by her only surviving son, Frank.[142] When she died in 1879, Frank continued the business for thirty-six years.

The Kleene brothers—Joseph and Victor—bought the Rephlo store before 1915.[143] Occupying the advantageous location where Missouri Boulevard intersects West Main Street, the Kleene brothers kept the store open another forty-five years, until Joseph retired in 1960.[144]

The Kleene brothers were born to German-speaking immigrants, Joseph Sr. and Margaret (Droste), who reared their children in the Mill Bottom neighborhood. Victor Kleene followed in his father's footsteps as a city alderman.[145]

Victor was described as having a "never-failing good nature" and the ability to "always come up smiling and [have] some word or expression to relieve a tense situation," Mayor Jesse Owen said.[146] Victor died unexpectedly in 1945, leaving the thirty-year-old business solely in the hands of his brother, Joseph Jr.

One of the last businesses to leave the Mill Bottom was the barbershop started by Henry Natsch in 1908 and continued by Oscar Hoffmeyer through 1975.[147]

Natsch was born in Missouri to Swiss immigrants and grew up on West Main Street at the turn of the twentieth century. By age twenty-one in 1908, he had opened his barbershop at 624 West Main Street.

After finishing barber college and a two-year apprenticeship in St. Louis, Hoffmeyer joined the Mill Bottom barbershop in 1925, when it was at 411 West Main Street.

At that time, the three blocks of West Main Street produced a "cacophony of sound," with loaded farmers' wagons lining up for Dulle's Mill, cattle being offloaded for the stockyards and the blacksmith's hammer ringing, Hoffmeyer recalled.[148]

The barbershop had a steady flow of working men leaving the railroad or the steamboat looking for not only a haircut and shave but also a hot-water bath. In the 1920s and 1930s, women were stopping in for haircuts too. And William Porter, a deaf man, worked as a shoe shiner there for twenty years.

When the Missouri Highway Patrol organized in the 1930s, patrolmen would drop off their Model A coupes and motorcycles at the main garage on West Main Street for maintenance, and then the officers would walk over to the barbershop to "get spruced up for duty," Hoffmeyer said.[149]

Natsch moved his barbershop to 503 West Main Street in 1929 and sold it to Hoffmeyer in 1941 before moving to Illinois to work at a U.S. Army ordnance plant.

Chapter 5

TRANSPORTATION

I n the early decades of Jefferson City, transportation was limited to one's own two feet, horsepower or the river.

Captain Jefferson T. Rogers established Rogers Landing at the foot of Harrison Street, next to his own impressive stone home, built on the edge of the Missouri River. It was the westernmost landing of the three in Jefferson City, the others being at the end of Jefferson Street and at the Missouri State Penitentiary.

In the earliest years of the Capital City, the river traffic was born: on canoes, keelboats, flatboats or French batteaux. The first steamboat to reach this far west, the *Independence*, passed by in 1819.[150]

The landing in the future Mill Bottom known as the Rogers Landing was first used by William Jones, likely the area's earliest white inhabitant. By 1822, Jones received a license from the Cole County Court to operate a ferry at the future north end of Harrison Street, where he kept a tavern. Jones was an early justice of the peace and city trustee, until he moved about 1829 and left the tavern and landing to his son, Robert Jones, who left about 1835.[151]

About that time, Rogers moved from the Callaway County side of the river to take over the landing. He and his father, Thomas Rogers, had carried freight and passengers across the Missouri River by horse-powered ferry for several years.[152]

In 1848, Rogers and partners E.B. Cordell, T.L Price and John Yount installed a steam ferry, which reduced the crossing to just three minutes. This technological upgrade improved north–south travelers' options for safely crossing the Missouri River.

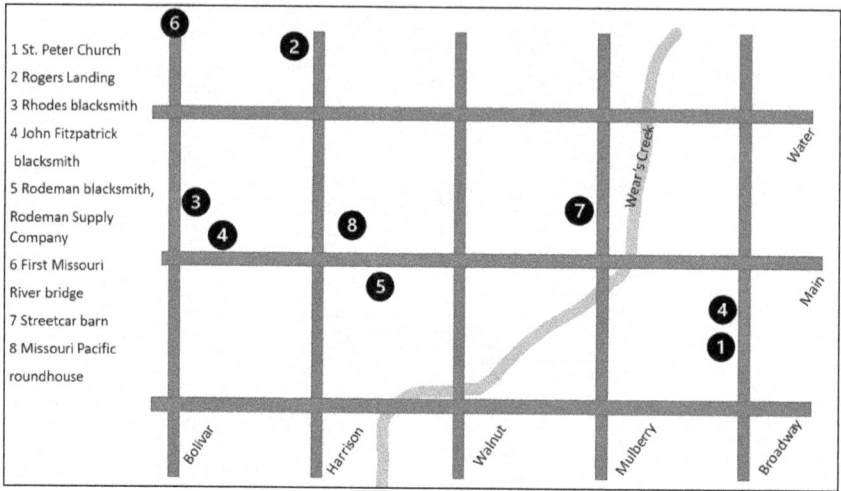

Map of early transportation in the Mill Bottom. *Map by Michelle and Stephen Brooks.*

Whether in his business, personal or professional dealings, Rogers was "progressive constantly, espousing measures calculated to make the community a better place to live."[153] Rogers helped many in distress over the years and served ten times as mayor, plus six as an alderman. He also helped rebuild the county fairgrounds after the Civil War and was strongly involved in enticing the railroad's development of the Mill Bottom.

The future Mill Bottom area was not only the location for ferry travelers to disembark but also the western entrance for travelers by horseback and wagon. That made having a blacksmith handy a necessity.

Wagons and horseshoes were a steady business. But when the Bruns-Dulle-Kroeger mill opened in the 1850s, bringing in farmers from the area, business increased. And many blacksmiths found work with the Missouri Pacific Railroad when it set up its shops and roundhouse in the 1860s.

One of the earliest blacksmiths, in what was then called the Goose Bottom, was opened as early as 1860 by John H. Kroeger, who also was partner with G.H. Dulle in the mill business. A man named Rhodes had a shop as early as 1867 near the northeast corner of Bolivar and Main Streets, which continued through the 1920s as a blacksmith's shop.

John F. Fitzpatrick opened a blacksmith and horseshoeing shop as early as 1863 with a partner as Fitzpatrick & Bowden, which dissolved in 1867.[154] The New Jersey–born blacksmith pre-made wagons and plows but had a reputation for his custom work, particularly repairs.[155]

John F. Fitzpatrick

—STILL IN THE—

FIELD!

Blacksmithing

AND

HORSE-SHOEING.

Wagons and Plows.

An 1873 advertisement for
blacksmith John F. Fitzpatrick.
Image courtesy of the Jefferson City
(MO) News Tribune.

By 1900, he had relocated his business from 210 Broadway to 626 West Main Street, closer to the railroad and mills, and partnered with his son, George. Here, the Richmond Hill Fire Company hung its bell.[156]

Known as "Fitz," Fitzpatrick was the first chief of the city fire department when it organized in 1871 with the purchase of the Silsby rotary steam pumper named the General E.L. Edwards.[157] During his fourteen years leading the fire department, he also served as a city alderman from 1873 to 1877 and from 1882 to 1883.[158]

The mainstay of smithing in the Mill Bottom was 519–521 West Main Street, where John Rodeman opened a blacksmith and wagon shop by 1892, while living across the street at 529 West Main Street. The shop had separate rooms for storage, wagon-making, painting, woodworking and smithing.

Born in Wardsville, Rodeman grew up in Jefferson City. He and his wife, Clara Amanda (Oncken), reared their six children at 214 Bolivar Street. Like most families in the Mill Bottom, the Rodemans belonged to St. Peter Catholic Church, where John was a charter member of the Helias Knights of Columbus.[159]

Rodeman Supply Company began "in a little shack across from the roundhouse" at 415 West Main Street.[160] Local lumber mogul Louis Ott helped John get established with a good credit rating on his first materials. Later, Ott would praise Rodeman as a "self-made man" in his weekly newspaper column, "Ott's Knot Hole."[161]

Rodeman was fortunate to have his son, Edward, follow in his footsteps.[162] They were part of an elite group of father-son businessmen who met annually to celebrate their family legacies. Others in the group included the Obermans, Tweedies, Dallmeyers, McHenrys, Otts and Mayers.[163]

One reason Rodeman's business survived more than a half century in the Mill Bottom was his ability to transition with the times. When the blacksmith business was no longer in demand and automobiles were becoming more common, he added parts and services for the latter. By 1930, he bought the lot next door to add additional floor space, due to exceptional growth.[164] The next year, Edward Rodeman took charge of the business.[165]

The Rodeman store ran weekly ads in the local newspaper showing the variety of its stock, which included hardware, automotive parts, farm machinery, restaurant supplies, heating units, beehives, dynamite and water decontamination tools.[166] The Rodeman motto was: "We have it, we can get it, or...it isn't made."[167]

In 1931, Rodeman celebrated the one hundredth anniversary of the McCormick reaper, invented by Cyrus Hall McCormick in 1831, with a luncheon, a display of an original reaper and a film shown for students. Before the McCormick reaper, a man could cut about 2.5 acres of wheat with a sickle and cradle per day. In 1931, a tractor-drawn tool could cut 20 acres per day.[168]

In 1934, the company made the news when it constructed a concrete, fireproof vault at its 417 West Main Street location.[169] The Rodeman company closed in 1958.[170]

The need for a bridge, rather than relying solely on ferry service, became apparent within the first decades of the Capital City. But it was seventy years before community organizers saw it realized.

The swing-style toll bridge opened in May 1896, funded solely with local contributions. The span left the north end of Bolivar Street, where the Rotary Centennial Park is today, and landed inside Callaway County.[171]

The steel bridge, designed by Kansas City bridge engineer J.A. Waddell and built by Leavenworth, Kansas builder A.J. Tullock, was dedicated with a parade of eighteen marching bands and a crowd of twenty thousand who poured in from excursion trains. The same day, the St. Louis Browns played an exhibition game versus the home team, and fireworks ended the evening.[172]

Waddell designed more than one thousand structures, more than one hundred of them movable, in the United States, Canada, Mexico, Russia, China, Japan and New Zealand. He set the standards for elevated railroad systems and developed suitable materials for large-span bridges. He invented the steam-powered high-lift bridge.[173]

Tullock, at his death in 1904, was one of the best-known bridge contractors in the West. He built up the Missouri Valley Bridge Company to prominence, building many of the largest bridges crossing the Missouri River.[174]

The Missouri Pacific Railroad had declined to build a bridge in 1893. That spurred more than one hundred Jefferson City residents to gather together with the common goal of seeing a bridge erected. From that movement, the Jefferson City Commercial Club, predecessor to today's Jefferson City Area Chamber of Commerce, was born.[175]

The first Missouri River Bridge opened in 1896, creating a boon to travelers and local businesses alike. *Photo courtesy of Missouri State Archives, Summers Collection.*

The $300,000 price tag (about $8.5 million in 2020) was covered solely by local pledges.[176] The original plan, and federal charter, was for a "high bridge" at Madison Street. But the designer determined immediately that this was impossible. Community leaders, including newspaperman Jake Fisher, urgently visited congressmen in Washington, D.C., to negotiate a new charter for a drawbridge at Bolivar Street.[177]

The bridge became a free road in 1932, when the private Jefferson Bridge and Transit Company was sold to the state. The remaining art deco pillars were added in 1934. The rest of the bridge was taken down in 1955, after the current southbound bridge opened. (The northbound bridge was added in 1991.)[178]

The Missouri River Bridge was originally made with a wooden road and wrought-iron handrails, 24 feet wide and 140 feet long.[179] When the trolley arrived in 1911, it was strengthened to carry the trolley and its freight and passenger business to North Jefferson City.[180]

Proposals for street railways had been made as early as 1891 but faced opposition from those who feared they would ruin streets, frighten horses, create noise and pollute the air.[181]

Mayor Cecil Thomas was known as "the builder" for the many infrastructure improvements he pushed along. Among those was the trolley car and the first High Street viaduct over Missouri Boulevard.

Waddell and Harrington of Kansas City laid the rails after local excavator Joseph Pope did the earthwork beginning in late 1910.[182]

The remaining trolley tracks were laid from Bolivar Street east on Main Street to Broadway, south on Broadway to High, east on High to Madison, north on Madison to Main, east on Main to Monroe, south on Monroe to High and to the original eastern terminus.[183]

The line was soon extended east on High Street to Ash Street, then further east to Clark, then south to Dunklin and finally further southeast to Moreland Avenue.[184] To the west, the line eventually rounded the water company and ended at Vista Place.[185]

Few streets were paved at the time, and "the old trolleys served a real need," recalled George Sherrell, a longtime driver.[186]

Four streetcars were met with fanfare when they arrived from St. Louis on March 16, 1911, and were taken to the barn behind the power company on West Main Street.[187]

The first to ride on April 1, 1911, on the new streetcar driven by Henry S. Beck, was Cecil Thomas, who was elected mayor the following year,

One of the more romantic pieces of Jefferson City history is the short-lived era of the trolleys. *Photo courtesy of Missouri State Archives, Summers Collection.*

Lawson Price, then-current mayor John Heinrichs and reporter Lawrence Lutkewitte, who would also take the first ride on the city bus that replaced the trolleys in November 1933.[188]

The orangish-yellow trolleys began regular service on April 2, 1911, Election Day. Two seats ran the length of each car, seating twenty and leaving room for another dozen to stand.[189] The motormen and conductors worked ten hours a day, seven days a week.

The only significant accident the streetcar service had was when a pair of mules hitched to a wagon on West Main Street ran in front of the trolley.[190]

In 1913, the McKinley System, which had one of the most successful electric railroads in the nation at the time, bought the Jefferson City Bridge and Transit Company, which owned the Missouri River Bridge, valued at more than $250,000, as well as the street railway.[191]

Eventually, the number of automobiles increased, and suburbs farther out were demanding service. Plus, the streetcars were causing damage to the paved streets.

As the streetcars put the horse and stagecoach out to pasture, so the bus with its rubber tires and without the limits of rails replaced the trolleys. What remained, however, was the Mill Bottom barn behind the power plant, originally built with four stalls for horses.

What may be the most iconic, if not romantic, piece of the Mill Bottom's lost architecture is the Missouri Pacific Railroad's roundhouse.

Many childhood memories are filled with mischievous visits to the repair shed when the engines were out or of visiting the workmen when they were in. What people remember today is the second roundhouse, built in 1901 with a turntable and well.[192]

The half-moon-shaped building in the 500 block of West Main Street had twenty stalls and was eighty-six feet long.[193] In the roundhouse's heyday, its 1901 doors were painted red.[194]

It served locomotives ranging from 1,400 to 2,200 horsepower until the end of steam power, which led to the roundhouse closing. After that, it was used for lumber and feed storage.[195] Then the building caught fire in the late 1970s and was demolished.

The first roundhouse on the site was built in 1871.[196]

In 1867, the Pacific Railroad set up a temporary shop with two turntables on land donated by the city in the 500 block of West Main Street.[197]

As late as 1871, the Pacific Railroad did not have a permanent shop between St. Louis and Pleasant Hill. Jefferson City was vying for that business against Sedalia and other towns along the rails.[198] The city had donated

The Missouri Pacific Railroad roundhouse was an icon for those who lived, worked and grew up in the Mill Bottom. *Photo courtesy of Missouri State Archives, Noe Collection.*

acres of choice land along the riverfront to the railroad on the condition that it build its machine shops there.[199]

After a financial crisis, the railroad company was reorganized in 1872 as the Missouri Pacific Railway.

The city's board of aldermen took out an injunction against the Pacific Railroad Company in 1873, preventing the latter from removing buildings and fixtures related to the roundhouse.[200] In 1874, the roundhouse was deemed abandoned by the city, which was hoping to transfer the property to a new railroad occupant.[201]

After being abandoned for several years, the railroad resumed use of the first roundhouse in 1875.[202] The old Missouri Pacific roundhouse was demolished in 1895.[203]

Activity increased in 1910, when the River Route from Jefferson City to Boonville was completed. In 1917, a merger with the St. Louis, Iron Mountain & Southern created the Missouri Pacific Railroad Company.[204]

In 1929, the railroad was one of the largest taxpayers in the Capital City, and many of its employees were homeowners and active in civic affairs. The railroad owned thirty-two acres of land along fourteen miles of track with fifty-eight buildings, including freight and passenger stations, roundhouse, offices, two modern coal chutes, storerooms, a telegraph office and tool houses.[205]

The first diesel engines were introduced in 1937, and by 1955 all steam engines had been retired, ending the need for most of the Jefferson City shops.[206]

PART II

THE FOOT

Chapter 6

BEFORE THE FOOT

L ittle architectural heritage remains of African American contributions or neighborhoods in the nineteenth century.

The Foot, once a more than six-block stretch of vitality and unique African American identity, did not develop until after Washington School, the public school for Black children, was built in 1903 in the 700 block of East Elm Street. Only after 1921, when Lincoln Institute became Lincoln University, did the neighborhood at "the Foot" of the campus hill see a significant growth in its middle class.

Before that, the majority of Black residents lived in the downtown area, along alleys—out of sight of the affluent white businesses but within walking distance of employment, most often domestic and labor-related.

VIOLET CLARK RAMSEY

What may have been the city's first uniquely African American neighborhood began with Violet Clark Ramsey's property in the 100 block of East Miller Street.

Brought to Jefferson City from Kentucky while she was enslaved, Violet Clark received her manumission papers from Ephraim Clark in 1838, when she was age forty-four, "for motives of benevolence and humanity."[207]

For the next twenty years, Violet Clark built a successful washing business. With the proceeds, she invested in real estate and bought the freedom of her husband, Elijah Eugah Ramsey Sr., and sons Elijah Jr. and Harrison.[208]

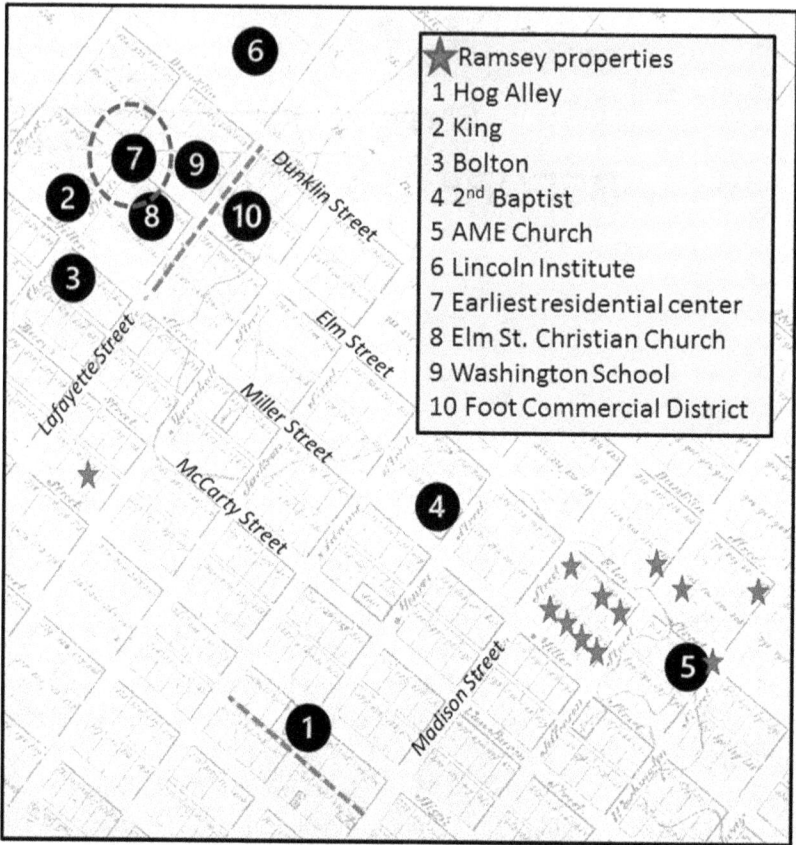

This map shows the early residential and cultural centers for African Americans in Jefferson City. *Map by Michelle Brooks.*

Six months after her emancipation, Violet Clark Ramsey bought her first piece of land at the southwest corner of Madison and Miller Streets for $200 (equivalent to nearly $3,000 in 2021) from white hotelier Henry Paulsel. Within two years, she also bought the adjacent lot for $300.[209]

At this corner, she built a log cabin, which served as her home and later housed the first worship services for the mission that became Quinn Chapel AME Church. Once Elijah Sr. was freed in 1845, his work as a drayman, teamster, farmer and laborer helped the couple acquire more property, including part of the 600 block of East High Street.[210]

The Ramseys bought three of the six remaining lots on the south side of the block on Miller Street, between Madison and Jefferson Streets, where the Central Motor Bank is today, and as founding members of Quinn Chapel, they donated part of the land for the first church building at 116 East Miller Street.[211]

The Ramseys also owned the two southside corner lots at Jefferson and Elm Streets and two lots at Washington and Dunklin Streets, where Prairie Farms Dairy and Coca-Cola Bottling Company are now.[212]

Well before the Civil War, the couple purchased a forty-acre farm south of the city, between today's Christy and Lorenzo Green Drives. This their son Harrison inherited, and in 1867, he conveyed the land to the Lincoln Institute Board of Trustees for $2,000.[213]

The Ramseys also owned another twenty acres south of the city, which developed into the Jefferson City High School and Pete Adkins Stadium.[214]

"Neither Violet, nor Elijah, could read or write, but they amassed a number of impressive real estate holdings, fulfilling their dreams against the odds," Nancy Thompson wrote in 2020.[215]

CHURCHES

Quinn Chapel was established in 1852 by the Reverend John Turner, meeting in the properties provided by the Ramseys. And in 1865, Second Baptist Church began meeting at its present site on the corner of Monroe and Miller Streets but in the former First Baptist Church meetinghouse.[216]

The Second Baptist Church was formed in 1859, when enslaved people were no longer welcome to worship with the white First Baptist Church. The new congregation first met in a small frame building near the corner of Jefferson Street and Capitol Avenue, then at the old Presbyterian building in the 100 block of Capitol Avenue, then at the corner of Monroe and Capitol.[217]

Because both of the early Black congregations in the 1860s chose the 100–200 blocks of East Miller Street, historian Gary Kremer said that this "indicated Blacks lived within easy walking distance."[218]

By 1877, nearly 75 percent of African Americans lived northwest of McCarty and Adams Streets. However, "the first hint of an emerging Black population concentration" was growing at the corner of Cherry and Elm Streets, Kremer said.[219]

In this area, oral tradition preserved the stories of other women like Violet Ramsey, who earned their freedom and bought property.[220]

MARTHA KING

In 1855, Martha King bought the lot at 501 Cherry Street, where the historic Hagan House stood before it was razed in 1982 to make way for city bus parking.[221] Christian Hagan built a modest, coarse limestone cottage, which had only two owners, both African American, during its 110-year existence.[222]

Sarah Bolton bought two lots nearby in 1863. And soon after the Civil War, Harriet Russell bought land near Bolton.[223]

By 1900, the homes of Black residents were more abundant south and east of McCarty and Adams Streets.[224] The highest concentration at that time was the 800 block of Elm and 700 block of Locust.

WASHINGTON SCHOOL

Two additions to Elm Street, between Lafayette and Cherry Streets, in 1903 reflected the shifting center of cultural identity: the Elm Street Community Christian Church and Washington School.[225]

Prior to Washington School, African American students attended classes in the 100 block of West McCarty Street. That pre–Civil War property became the segregated schoolhouse in 1875. Before that, public school classes for Jefferson City's African American students were taught at the "House on Hobo Hill," where the former Simonsen Ninth Grade Center stands today.

The very first school for African American students was privately operated by the American Missionary Association in 1864–65, when it was still illegal in Missouri to teach African Americans, free or enslaved, to read or write. Lydia Hess Montague taught the first classes to both young and old.

Lincoln Institute began in September 1866, under white Lieutenant Richard Baxter Foster, one of the founders from the Sixty-Second U.S. Colored Troops. In 1867, Foster was hired by the public school to teach the local African American children. Then classes moved to the West McCarty Street location in 1875.

By 1908, the Foot was developing into the center of a uniquely African American, working-class neighborhood. About two dozen families lived along the 400–600 blocks of Lafayette Street. By 1913, nearly thirty families made their homes in just the 600 block of Lafayette. Early businesses

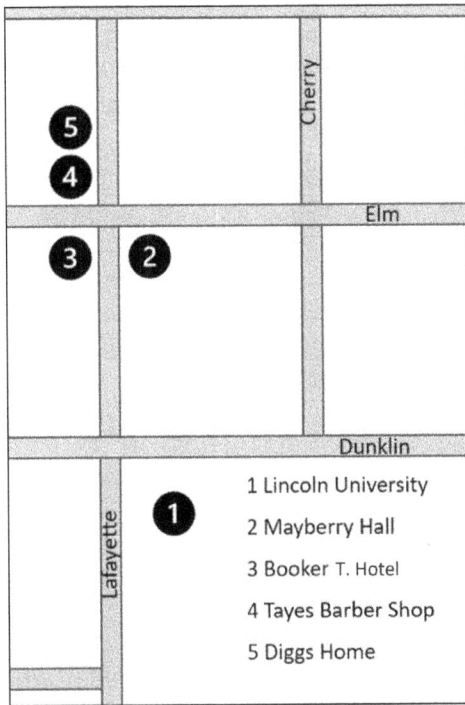

1 Lincoln University
2 Mayberry Hall
3 Booker T. Hotel
4 Tayes Barber Shop
5 Diggs Home

Map of the earliest anchors for the Foot neighborhood. *Map by Michelle and Stephen Brooks.*

established there included Duke Diggs moving company, a grocery store, several cafés and a dry cleaner.[226]

Kremer notes that by 1921, Jefferson City, for the first time, was becoming segregated. For two-thirds of the African American homes, that meant living in poorly accessible homes without basic utilities.[227]

Like elsewhere across the United States at the time, many white-owned businesses denied service based on skin color. Segregation, then, also created opportunities for Black entrepreneurs to open stores and offer services, with a ready customer base in the Foot.

MARTIN MAYBERRY

One of the earliest African American entrepreneurs was Martin Mayberry, who opened a restaurant and grocery store by 1900 at 601 Lafayette Street.[228] He later expanded the Capitol City Mercantile Company into 603 and 605 Lafayette Street.

Born in Murray County, Tennessee, Martin David Mayberry farmed in Mississippi before moving to Osage City about 1887.[229] He and Anna (Church) had six children, including Charles, who continued to farm in Osage City when his father moved to Jefferson City.

"Mayberry Hall," as the structure spanning 601–605 Lafayette Street was known, was the site of early social gatherings and political club rallies, both Republican and Democrat, through the 1930s.[230] Comie Gathright set up a barbershop with a billiard parlor in the rear of 601 Lafayette Street. Queenie Mayberry, daughter-in-law to Martin, opened a restaurant in 603, which later became William Hardiman's barbershop. And in 605 Lafayette, Cordelia Rutledge had a restaurant with billiards.

B.F. KING

Another of the earliest residents in this future historic neighborhood was Benjamin Franklin King. Born in Ohio, he moved his family from Tennessee to Jefferson City in 1899 for work as a superintendent at the Hoskins-Ross Broom Manufacturing Company. Also known as the Central Broom Company, it hired seventy-five inmates from the Missouri State Penitentiary to work at 530 State Street, which later became Shryack-Hirst Grocery Company's warehouse.

The King family built a substantial home at 726 Lafayette Street, where Benjamin's wife, Ida Lee (Crowley), and children remained after his death in 1922. The Mayberry family built a hotel at 600 Lafayette Street, where Ida Lee King operated a grocery store. For a time, she also was a matron for Lincoln University.

Their son, Guy McKinley King, helped with the grocery business through the 1930s. A World War I veteran, Guy King served as a mechanic in France with the Colored Headquarter Company of the 809th Pioneer Infantry. When the Toney Jenkins American Legion Post organized with fifteen members on February 1, 1934, at the old community center building, 901 East Dunklin Street, Guy King was its first commander.

"As the black community became more concentrated in that part of town, more black entrepreneurs set up shop there," Kremer said.[231]

Chapter 7

TURNING POINT

Whe Lincoln Institute became Lincoln University in 1921, it marked a turning point, not only for the university but also for the burgeoning neighborhood at the foot of the hilltop campus. University presidents Nathan Young and C.W. Florence both made attracting better-qualified instructors a priority. Improving salaries was one way to do that. And that had a trickle-down impact on the rest of the African American community. One result was "a class of professionals who could afford to buy houses," historian Gary Kremer observed.[232]

When Representative Walthall Moore of St. Louis arrived in 1921 in Jefferson City as the first elected African American to serve as a state representative, he likely slept on the Lincoln campus, as no white hotels in the city would serve him.[233]

HOTEL

Only a few years later, the Mayberry family would resolve this issue with the Mayberry Hotel on the second floor at 600 Lafayette Street, where Queenie Mayberry operated a restaurant, and originally Ida and Benjamin King, then Guy King, operated a grocery on the main level. The third floor was designed for a theater, and the basement became an entertainment hot spot.[234]

Like his father, Martin, Charlie Mayberry moved to Jefferson City from Osage City, where he had owned a lot of property. According to contemporary business owner Kenneth Logan, Mayberry similarly bought a lot of property in the Lafayette and Elm area. But the younger Mayberry took out a blanket mortgage on all of his property to build the hotel. When he defaulted, Ott Lumber Company, which had been hired to build the three-story brick hotel, confiscated all of it.[235]

William Moore took over the hotel operations about 1930, and through the 1940s, it became known as the Lincoln Hotel under the ownership of white Murphy Clark, later a railroad and prison worker. During that decade, Guy King continued the grocery business and the restaurant changed hands several times.

The Lincoln Hotel was the only listing for Jefferson City in the 1941 *Negro Motorist Green Book*, printed by Victor Green.[236]

By 1945, when Leo Daniels renovated the hotel, it had gained the name of the Booker T. "I am striving to maintain a high standard of decorum," Daniels told the *Clarion* in 1945.[237]

According to the *Green Book* in the 1940s, the other accommodations for Black travelers through Jefferson City at the time were tourist homes, at Miss C. Wooldridge's home at 418 Adams Street or at R. Graves' home at 314 East Dunklin Street.[238]

A white man from southeast Missouri, Daniels came to Jefferson City in 1943 as a printing clerk for the state, a job from which he resigned to keep the hotel. He began working for the *Daily American* newspaper in Poplar Bluff at age fourteen, and later in life, he published two newspapers, which his family had owned for more than fifty years. He also served three terms as state representative from Reynolds County.

In just a few weeks after Daniels' makeover, the thirty-five-room hotel was filled to capacity on weekends.[239]

The main floor had twenty-five booths with pink walls and drapes, white curtains, a sky-blue ceiling and more tables in the center. Above each booth was a picture of an African American celebrity.[240] It was often the gathering place for community groups.[241] Hotel rooms were on the second floor, and the third floor was reserved as a dormitory for servicemen.[242]

The basement had nineteen booths and a seating capacity of 150, as well as a dance floor and an orchestra stand frequently occupied by the university's Lincoln Collegians band. By student suggestion, Daniels called the downstairs venue "the Subway."[243]

The large building also served as the cab stand, and a barbershop also was in the basement.

The Booker T. Hotel, also known as the Lincoln Hotel and the Mayberry Hotel, was a central point in the life and events of the Foot for forty years. *Photo courtesy of Janet Maurer.*

Behind the hotel lived an old man named "Alley Oop," like the song, who lived in a cardboard house he built next to a tree, recalled former resident Eric Kelley.[244]

When Rufus Petty took over the hotel in 1953, he gave the property another facelift and renamed it the Carver Hotel.[245] During that time, the restaurant was under Hazel Kirkpatrick.

Petty was born in Mississippi and was working for the railroad in Butler County when he enlisted with the 805th Pioneer Infantry, an all-Black regiment, during World War I, serving in Europe 1918–19.[246] By 1930, he was a janitor at the capitol and then a truck driver for the Ott Lumber Company, boarding at 513 Lafayette Street with Annie Mayberry.[247]

Petty was active in Second Baptist Church; the local NAACP; the Toney Jenkins American Legion Post, where he was a post commander; and the Jefferson City Community Center Association. Petty also was an active Republican, serving as neighborhood election judge and state convention delegate. Before opening the Carver Hotel, he was a clerk at the capitol.[248]

The hotel caught fire in 1965, when it was used by many students for off-campus residences. Though not lost then, it was razed in 1966 as part of the Jefferson City Housing Authority's Campus View Urban Renewal.

COMMERCIAL DEVELOPMENT

In the 1920s, the Foot commercial district was just taking shape at the intersection of Elm and Lafayette Streets with the hotel at the center.

On the west side of the 500 block, directly underneath today's overpass, Duke Diggs had set up his home and moving and storage company at 526 Lafayette Street.

Artist-barber Ulysses Grant Tayes worked from his home next door to Diggs at 528, where Lannie Hall added a tailor shop and Jack King set up a shoe shine business.

The commercial district stretched further south, adding two restaurants at 614 and 626 Lafayette Street: the Roy Graham Lunchroom and another operated by Martin Moseley.

And by the end of the 1920s, Benjamin H. Logan had built a home at 524 Lafayette Street, on the other side of Duke Diggs' home, where he opened a shoe repair shop.

Two cab companies were in operation: Henry B. Burton operated out of 628 Lafayette, which also was the Lincoln Lunchroom, and Charles Mayberry established the Veteran's Cab Company at his restaurant at 600 Lafayette.

DUKE AND ESTELLA DIGGS

Duke Diggs purchased part of the 500 block of Lafayette Street in the late 1890s and more after the turn of the century. When he built his large brick home about 1920, he dismantled and moved a small frame home, where Peggy Williams' mother was born.[249]

"That was a big house! It had an attic and everything," Williams, a former resident, recalled of the Diggs home. The back porch had a swing overlooking Weir's Creek, and it had a garage for one of the few cars in the neighborhood at the time.[250] Another former resident, Perry Douglas, remembered the car as a black Packard Clipper.[251]

Diggs and his wife, Estella (Branham), did not have children but allowed the neighborhood children to play behind their house, Williams recalled. The Diggs house was the location for early lodge meetings, and with four bedrooms, they could board visiting dignitaries.[252]

"It's disgraceful that it was torn down and not kept as an historic place," Douglas said.[253]

TAYES BARBER SHOP

Diggs' neighbor, Ulysses S. Grant Tayes, was called "Baby Tayes."[254] His one-and-one-half-story frame house was built about 1895, long before Diggs built his.[255] By the end of the barbershop's life, it was known to lean to the north and shook when people walked across the floor.[256]

Tayes Barber Shop "was where all the old guys would go sit and talk about the neighborhood. If you wanted to know anything, you went to the barbershop," former resident Glover Brown Jr. said.[257]

The entrance to the Tayes Barber Shop had a sign saying: "Tayes Art Museum Admission Free." At any moment, Tayes might reach for the piano inside his shop to play a tune.[258]

Although Tayes earned fourteen medals and prizes for his artwork, he never received formal training. And his craft as a violinist and pianist came by ear, not by lesson.[259]

Most of his work was on display in his Lafayette Street shop, including his first award winner, *Portrait of a Child*, which received the Urban League Art Museum's first prize in 1923.[260] His work was exhibited by the Harmon Foundation, Atlanta University, the St. Louis Public Library, the St. Louis Artists Guild, Artist League, Urban League and Lincoln University.[261] He was included in the 1999 *Who Was Who in American Art* collection.[262]

Tayes "likes to paint from life and prefers portraiture...dark backgrounds in the manner of the old masters," reporter Raymond Tisby wrote for the *Clarion* in 1953. Mostly, Tayes drew upon life and times in the Foot for his artwork, including the better-known *Barber Shop* (1947) and *Bar Scene* (1950).[263]

Tayes picked up the wonder of art in his hometown of Warrensburg, where he watched the white children of Erma Cheatham paint while his mother cleaned their home.[264]

"I was irresistibly drawn to it," Tayes told the *Jefferson City Post Tribune* in 1931.[265]

Warrensburg artist Walter Hout and Cheatham supported Tayes' interest and his desire for higher education by securing a job for him in Jefferson City. As house boy to chief justice of the Missouri Supreme Court John R. Green, Tayes began his studies at Lincoln Institute in 1904.[266] Later, he worked as a waiter at the Monroe House.[267]

Tayes completed three degrees from Lincoln: a sixty-hour degree in 1908, a ninety-hour degree in 1921 and a Bachelor of Arts degree in education in 1936. He was a lifelong teacher, but he taught formally for twenty-three years in schools including Pacific, DeSoto, Crystal City, Eldon, Paris and Dalton.[268]

By 1921, he and his second wife, Laura Alice (Jackson), had moved to 528 Lafayette, where she lived until her death in 1942.[269] There they reared their daughter, Mildred Beatrice, born in 1913. Tayes first married Mary Aline Lane, who died in 1911; later, he married Lillian Lee, who preceded him in death in 1948.

Throughout his life, barbering and music kept Tayes' wallet and his social life full. The barbering he learned at age twelve, after working in a Warrensburg barbershop as a shoe shiner.[270] And during several years in St. Louis, he operated the U.S. Barber Shop at 325 Pine Street while picking up evening gigs.[271] He played his piano on St. Louis radio stations, including KMOX, and early on at the local KWOS station.[272]

Tayes also wrote occasional pieces for the *St. Louis Argus* and other publications, including a philosophical and humorous column titled "Oh, Tempora."[273]

He was "one of the most colorful and illustrious Lincoln University graduates," Raymond Tisby wrote in the *Lincoln Clarion* in 1953.[274]

Chapter 8

EMERGING

nto the 1930s, the Foot truly came into its own, with additional services like Logan's Shoe Repair and professionals like Dr. Reginald Richardson. The hotel and its basement venue drew in many of the noted national Black figures of the day, especially those traveling across the state between its metro cities.

The Subway in the Booker T. went by other names over the decades, including the Green Onion and El Grotto; it was a popular stop for Black entertainers.[275] Across Lafayette Street, the El Dorado Club was behind Jack King's Drug Store, and the Lonestar Club was just a few blocks east on Elm Street.

Performers like Louis Rivera and his Trio brought popular music into the small community.[276] Glover Brown Jr., who grew up on the Foot with his parents operating the Tops Restaurant on the south end of the same block as the hotel, remembered several famous performers who would eat at his parents' restaurant while traveling through.[277]

Jazz musician Louis Armstrong took a liking to a local girl while here, and Miss Chi from the Ikettes enjoyed Glover Brown Sr.'s barbecue. Ray Charles performed and stayed in the Foot, as did Ike and Tina Turner.[278]

Other famous African American travelers stayed at the hotel and ate at the restaurants on the Foot in those days. Arthur Brown, another son of the Tops owners, remembered meeting professional basketball player Wilt Chamberlain and pro tennis champion Arthur Ashe.[279] Don Webb, stepson of the Tops owner, remembered seeing circus performers and the Harlem Globetrotters.

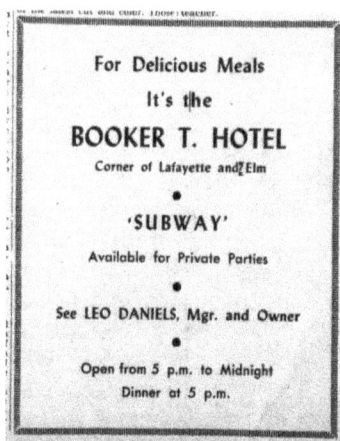

For Delicious Meals

It's the

BOOKER T. HOTEL

Corner of Lafayette and Elm

•

'SUBWAY'

Available for Private Parties

•

See LEO DANIELS, Mgr. and Owner

•

Open from 5 p.m. to Midnight

Dinner at 5 p.m.

Advertising in the 1945 *Lincoln Clarion* for the Subway in the basement of the Booker T. Hotel. *Photo courtesy of Lincoln University Archives.*

The hotel also allowed special guests of the campus to have a place to stay, including Bill Cosby, the Reverend Jesse Jackson and Dr. Martin Luther King Jr.'s children.[280]

Notable Lincoln alumni who returned and stayed in the Foot included Fifth Dimension member Ron Townson, who also had been a member of Second Baptist Church, and comedian Joe Torre, who played football at Lincoln.[281]

Community members, as well as students and faculty from Lincoln University, would gather at the Subway or the hotel's restaurant. However, many who grew up in the neighborhood remember being warned as children not to go near the Booker T. or the Subway at night.[282]

This was a favorite hangout, especially for professors of the Harlem Renaissance. Poet Sterling Brown was one of the first Harvard-trained professors attracted to Lincoln after it attained university status.[283]

Brown was interested in folk culture, folk art and the blues, "not the more high-brow, but the vernacular," said historian Gary Kremer. At this time, "Lincoln disallowed the playing of the blues."[284]

"As I've read about it, Sterling Brown was always in hot water with the administration because what he wanted to do was hang out in the dives, hang out in the Booker T. Hotel, and he wrote a lot of poetry. He only stayed two years…But some of his most famous poems are written about the Foot," Kremer said.[285]

The poem series about "Slim Greer" was based on a waiter at the hotel restaurant. And Brown's poem "Checkers" is about two men playing checkers every Saturday night outside a local barbershop.[286]

While the clubs and hotel provided entertainment and a safe place for travelers, other professionals were making the Foot their home and setting up businesses.

DR. REGINALD RICHARDSON

An immigrant from St. Martin in the British West Indies, Dr. Reginald Granvilla Richardson moved to Jefferson City in the late 1920s, making his home and office at 421 Lafayette Street. He attended Howard University in Washington, D.C., where he met his wife, Nana (Jones).[287]

Richardson was the longtime university physician and later was on staff at St. Mary's Hospital.[288] He was acutely aware of community health and was involved in community betterment, including service as president of the Negro Chamber of Commerce.[289]

But it was his wife, Nana, who had the "unusual distinction of organizing Jefferson City's six Negro women's clubs," a 1950 *Clarion* story said. Those were the Modern Priscilla Art and Charity Club, Civic Pride Charity Club, Needlecraft Art and Charity Club, OME Charity Club, Progressive Art and Charity Club and Community Helper's Club.[290]

Dr. Richardson may have been the first Black physician to open a practice in the Foot, but Dr. Herbert Everett Johnson may have been the first African American to practice medicine in Jefferson City, arriving by 1914 and opening an office at 215 Jefferson Street.[291]

Several other early African American physicians followed Richardson, including William Arthur and Stanley Daigle in the 1940s.[292]

DR. WILLIAM ROSS

Dr. William Ross, whose home office still survives at 500 Lafayette Street, arrived in the 1950s, practicing for fifty-three years, including as the university's director of health services.[293]

An advocate for equal rights, Ross not only cared for all races in his medical practice but also marched in the historic 1962 Selma-to-Montgomery, Alabama, civil rights action with Martin Luther King Jr. During the Vietnam War era, he also advocated for larger draft boards to ensure Black men were not disproportionately drafted for military service.[294]

During his thirty-five years as president of the local NAACP branch, Dr. Ross "was instrumental in the racial integration of the Missouri State Highway Patrol, as well as local establishments, like the…golf course, skating rink, swimming pools and theaters," an informational panel said.[295]

Dr. Charles Cooper, a Lincoln alumnus, earned his Doctor of Medicine from Meharry Medical College, a historically Black medical school in Nashville, Tennessee. He began his family practice in Jefferson City in 1967 at 423 Cherry Street, then moved in the 1980s to the southeast corner of Dunklin and Monroe Streets.[296]

LOGAN'S SHOE REPAIR

One of the longest-running businesses in the Foot was Logan's Shoe Repair, or Nu-Way Shoe.[297] Benjamin Harrison Logan was the grandson of one of the founding soldiers of Lincoln University.[298] Born in New Bloomfield, Logan graduated with a certificate in shoe repair from Lincoln when it was still Lincoln Institute, in 1914. He made shoes for soldiers during World War I and then opened his first shop at 610 Lafayette Street in 1919.

The Logan Shoe Repair Store moved in 1925 into the Logan home at 524 Lafayette, where Logan's wife, Eula (Sanders)—a Jefferson City native who also held Lincoln certificates in music and home economics—could watch the business while he worked a second job as custodian for white downtown businesses.[299]

Their son Kenneth started at Washington School at age four and finished grade school at thirteen and high school at sixteen. After three years as an English and French major, the younger Logan realized he preferred working with his hands and went to work in his father's shop about 1938. Kenneth's brother, Herbert "Cab" Logan, advanced from custodian to become the first Black vice president at Exchange Bank.[300]

The Logan shop was narrow, with all kinds of machinery. They attached metal plates on the heels and toes of customers' shoes to extend their life and custom-made corrective shoes. The Logans bought their leather and supplies in California, Missouri.[301]

Kenneth Logan took over the family business about 1957, repairing shoes for more than seventy years until the day he died. His favorite part of the business was making custom-made shoes, even special shoes to help correct crooked legs. The younger Logan said his job was fun and he enjoyed making people feel better.[302]

"I enjoy life and I enjoy people," he said.[303]

When the first overpass was built at Lafayette Street and Whitton Expressway, Logan, along with others, lost his home and business. In 1958,

Kenneth Logan took over the family business of shoe repair in the Foot from his father, Benjamin, and continued it for seventy years, despite being relocated due to urban renewal. *Photo courtesy of Joyce Logan Webb.*

he built a new home in the 700 block of Jackson Street and moved his shop to the northeast corner of Lafayette and Dunklin Streets, where Rogers' Sundries once was.[304]

Clifford "Wingy" Dameron converted the building into apartments and a pool hall, with the shoe shop next door. When Wingy's closed in 1962, Logan's shoe repair moved into Pohl's Shoe Store on the South Side. When Pohl's closed in 1995, he joined Dave Gilmore's saddle shop on East High Street.[305]

"Daddy loved to visit with people; he loved to be down at the shop," his daughter Joyce Logan Webb said.[306]

Jack King

Another early entrepreneur in the Foot was Jack Wilson King. Born in Guthrie, he moved to Jefferson City to work in a bakery and as a deliveryman. By 1925, he was a bootblack at Tayes Barber Shop, 528 Lafayette Street, then added a taxi service from the same place in the early 1930s.

About 1936, he opened a tavern called Jack's Place at 605 Lafayette Street, which he converted about 1942 into a drugstore and kept for twenty-three years.[307] From his vantage in the neighborhood, King was sometimes victim or witness of crimes.

In 1933, Jefferson City police chief John Bruner followed a national trend, assigning a Black officer to the African American neighborhood. However, at this time, police officers were appointed more for their political influence than their training and experience.[308]

Officer Wallace Lawson

Wallace Lawson, a well-liked barbecue man, was first appointed police officer to the African American neighborhood in April 1933 and then reappointed.[309] Born in Jefferson City, he had worked as a farmer and laborer before joining the police.

Lawson became the first policeman in Jefferson City killed in the line of duty. James Turner had caused a ruckus at Bill's Café on Lafayette Street, to which Lawson responded. The pair exchanged threats, and Lawson advised Turner to go home. The officer followed Turner, and when he arrived at his front porch, the subject fired two shots from a shotgun, killing Lawson almost instantly.[310]

The city council considered not replacing Lawson with another African American officer but was persuaded to continue the practice by Lincoln professor John W. Damel.[311]

Sergeant Booker Mason

Booker Mason, a drugstore porter born in Chamois, was appointed to replace Lawson. Just three years after Lawson was shot, Mason also was involved in a shooting. Bill Griffin, the chauffeur for Mayor Means Ray, had a reputation as a troublemaker. One night, Griffin was hanging with some regulars at Tayes Barber Shop when Mason walked by. Griffin shouted that he was going to take the policeman's job.[312]

The police officer continued walking, and Griffin followed, taking Mason by the shoulder, swinging him around and striking him. When Mason backed off, Griffin lunged at him, cutting the officer's hand with a pocketknife. At the same time, Mason fired his "heavy service revolver" into Griffin's left breast, killing him.[313]

By the 1940s, Mason was a pistol champion among the Jefferson City police officers.[314] For twenty years, he responded to assaults, burglaries and other crimes in the Lafayette Street area, and he helped recover escaped convicts and suspects from other cities who were hiding in the Foot.

Mason also was a fixture in the community, serving as a judge for contests, working with the NAACP and singing with Zeke Bagby and his Four Harmony Boys.[315]

When the city police department reorganized in 1957, Mason was the first Black sergeant. At Mason's death the following year, Police Chief Claude Short said, "Booker's death leaves a gap in the force I can't fill. He was a good officer—one that I could always depend on."[316]

Chapter 9

SERVICE

In a segregated Jefferson City, another essential service in the Foot was taxi service.

As early as 1929, Charles R. Mayberry Sr. had opened the Veteran's Cab Company at his hotel at 600 Lafayette Street, and Henry Burton ran one from 628 Lafayette Street. Others that followed included Jack King at 528 Lafayette Street, Capital Cab Company from 806 Lafayette Street and Kunz 25 Cent Cab Company from the corner of Miller and Linn Streets.

Mayberry's son-in-law, Norman Bolton Sr., was the neighborhood taxi driver by 1940, living at 515 Lafayette Street. Before marrying Ethel (Mayberry), Bolton had been a truck driver for Decker Ramsey Company and a purchasing agent at the state capitol.

After returning from World War II, Charles R. "Bob" Mayberry Jr. "realized the dire need and opportunities for Negro cabs in this city," reporter William Bailey wrote for the *Lincoln Clarion* in 1947. White cab drivers took advantage of their monopoly, being tardy for African American pickups and evicting Black riders to make room for white passengers. For example, "a Negro woman sharing the cab with a white passenger [had been] forced to ride in the front seat with the luggage crowded in around her."[317]

At first, Bob Mayberry was refused a city cab license several times, but he persisted as an honorably discharged veteran.[318] He opened the Courteous Cab Company out of 505 Lafayette Street in 1946.[319]

Bob Mayberry was a corporal in the 279th Quartermaster Battalion. As a supply clerk, he was part of the campaigns into northern France, Germany

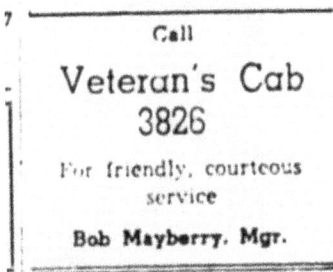

Advertising in the 1947 *Lincoln Clarion* for Veteran's Cab under Bob Mayberry as manager. *Photo courtesy of Lincoln University Archives.*

and Normandy, for which he received three Bronze Stars.[320] Before his service, he had been a janitor in the state liquor control division at the Broadway State Office Building.[321]

The next year, Bob Mayberry and fellow veterans reorganized as the Veteran's Cab Company, operating four cars twenty-four hours a day out of Mayberry Hall at 601–605 Lafayette Street.

Hulan Henderson, Norman Bolton Sr., William Avery and Bob Mayberry were popular drivers. Other early organizers included Norman Bolton Jr., James Davis, Paul Gilmore, Leonard Foster and Frances Crews.[322]

Henderson was born in Fulton, where he was a taxi driver before and after World War II.[323] He left Fulton about 1946, after a white woman sued another white man for "associating her name" with Henderson.[324] Hulen's Taxi Stand was remembered by those who grew up in the area of the Foot as a slender retail space with six stools and just enough room to buy a soda.[325]

Avery, originally from Clinton, was a truck driver before the war and then also with the 1505th U.S. Army Air Force Base Unit at Mather Field, California.

Well-known cabbie Norman Bolton Sr. later replaced his brother-in-law, Bob Mayberry, as the director of the Veteran's Cab Company and moved the operation back to his home at 515 Lafayette Street.[326]

Bolton Sr. was born in Osage County, moving to Jefferson City as a child to live with his grandparents. He worked for Decker Ramsey Company before World War I and then as a chauffeur.[327]

His son, Norman Bolton Jr., served in World War II, but died at age thirty-one in a car accident. His grandson, Robert Marcus Bolton, graduated from the U.S. Air Force Academy.

When Bolton joined the Jefferson City police department in 1949 with Charles Robinson, replacing Herbert Bagby and Booker Mason, he was "well-known to Lincoln students as the genial taxi driver," the *Clarion* reported.[328]

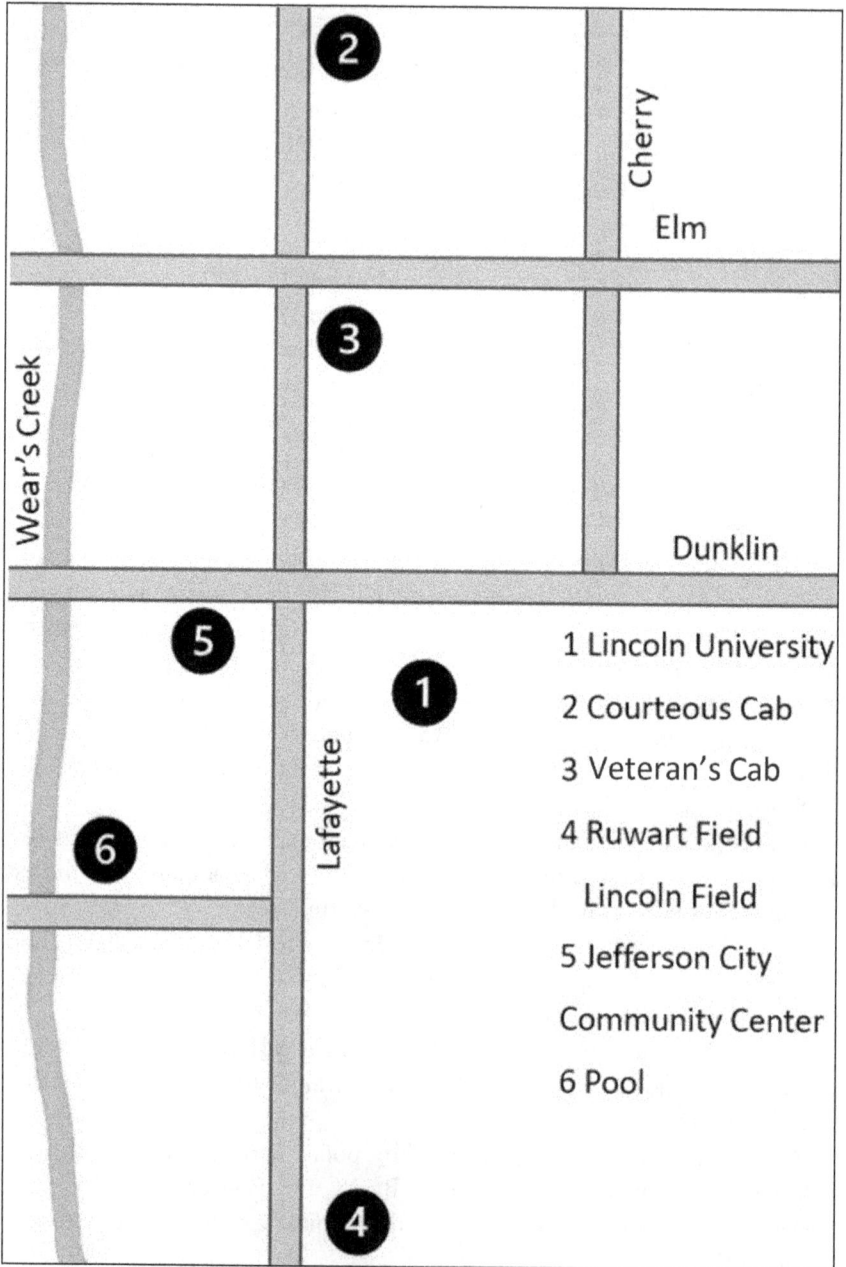

Map of the Foot amenities. *Map by Michelle and Stephen Brooks.*

CHARLES ROBINSON

Like many of the returning veterans, policemen and cab drivers, Bolton was part of the baseball culture. He was both a player and manager for the Mohawks baseball team.[329]

The Mohawks were the premier local team for Black players, replacing the Hubs, which had preferred more skilled players from out of town over local talent. The Mohawks were organized in 1922 by Charles "Lefty" Robinson, a longtime left-handed pitcher and manager with the Mohawks.[330]

The Mohawks played at the board fence–enclosed Ruwart Field, which became the Lincoln practice field.[331] At one time they were the "kings" of Jefferson City baseball.

In 1923, Robinson instigated a deal with teams from the American Negro Baseball League, including the Kansas City Monarchs, St. Louis Stars, Birmingham Black Barons and a team from Cuba. These exhibition games were a benefit to the professional teams, traveling between metropolitan cities, as well local crowd-pleasers.

Early team members included center-fielder Bud Rankin, shortstop Willie Smith, Robinson, left-fielder Fred Hull, second baseman Booker Mason, Leroy Groves, Guy King, pitcher Julius Mulky, first baseman H.J. Graves, utility player Buck Coden, catcher Ralph "Pepper" Price and utility player Hubert Smith.

Robinson had been invited to pitch for the professional St. Louis Stars in 1924. But after one month, he returned, preferring to be close to his family and make more money working at the capitol.[332]

"I learned to throw the curve by watching a crippled man in my hometown of New London—something was wrong with his hand and his thumb stuck straight up in the air," Robinson said. But he eventually had to learn to throw the curve ball the right way, as batters learned to anticipate the curveball when they saw his thumb up.[333]

In the community, Robinson served fifteen years as president of the Jefferson City Community Center Association and was the last surviving charter member of the local NAACP chapter, for which he served twenty-seven years as chapter treasurer.

After the community center was completed in 1942, Robinson was vocal for further improvements to the Black community, including a swimming pool and the rerouting of Weir's Creek, both of which came to fruition by 1950.[334] He also was instrumental in creating a nursery school for working mothers and the Teen Town program.[335]

Robinson was active in the Republican Party, serving as delegate to the 1960 national convention and becoming the first Black man in modern times to be a candidate for city office, losing in 1961 to the incumbent city assessor.[336]

In 1966, Robinson spoke up at a Jefferson City Public Schools board meeting after no one from the African American community was named to a bond issue committee, saying, "It's not going to hurt you to get a little color into this affair."[337] He suggested Dr. Charles Hoard, dean of students at Lincoln, and was applauded when he sat down at the meeting.

Robinson came to Jefferson City in 1912 from New London to work in the Governor Arthur Hyde administration, and in 1922, he was the first Black employee for the State Workmen's Compensation Commission. After working for the food and drug department and the state senate, he worked at Lincoln in the 1950s before becoming a funeral director with Dulle Funeral Home.[338]

At his death in 1974, Governor Christopher Bond proclaimed a Charles E. Robinson Day. And the city's JeffTran headquarters at 820 East Miller Street was named in his honor.[339]

Chapter 10

KEY INGREDIENT

O ne of the key ingredients to the Foot's unique identity was its food. Whether it was Washington School students coming down the hill for a hot dog and potato chips from Turner's gas station or visitors stopping for a plate of barbecue at the Tops, the tastes and locations are shared memories for hundreds who lived, worked, studied or played in the neighborhood.

LEONA RICE

Leona Rice may be one of the best remembered. She opened Leona's Sandwich Shop in 1950 at 603 Lafayette Street, replacing Norman Bolton's Veterans Lunch Room. A decade later, she opened a second location, Leona's Café, in the Booker T. Hotel and operated both until urban renewal closed her business.[340]

Rice provided jobs for many of the Lincoln students who otherwise could not have completed their education. And she fed many students, whether they could pay at the time or not. Later, some of these students paid her back, and others paid her back with kindness.[341]

"She had a heart of gold...fed you whether you were hungry or not, or [whether] you could pay or not," recalled Perry Douglas.[342]

Leona Rice earned the nickname "Mama" for her generosity and kindness, feeding Lincoln students—whether or not they could pay—at her Lafayette Street restaurant. When urban renewal ended the restaurant, she moved her home-cooked meals onto campus. *Photo courtesy of Lincoln University Archives.*

By 1956, Rice had earned the moniker of "Mama" due to her generosity.[343] Her menu included breakfast and sandwiches, pies and soup, steak and chicken. Arthur Brown remembers fondly Leona's chili mac: spaghetti noodles with meat and cheese and a big frankfurter with mustard on top.[344]

For a year after the Booker T. Hotel, and her restaurant with it, was torn down in 1966, Rice was out of work.[345] Then, after years of Lincoln students and faculty coming to her, she went to them.

Rice operated the snack shop in Scruggs Student Union before it was burned in 1969. Then she was the first to open the dining room when Dawson Hall opened in 1972. Next, she moved to the new student center, where she fixed all of the meals in the café. Lastly, she ran Mom's Place, a restaurant in the back of the student dining room.[346]

Leona Rice was married to U.S. Army veteran, police officer and human rights advocate William Rice. They lived in a green and white house south of the Booker T. before urban renewal claimed it, too.[347]

The restaurant at the cornerstone hotel had changed hands several times from 1921 to 1966. Charles and Queenie Mayberry, the hotel's first owners, operated the restaurant through the 1920s. In the 1930s, James Blankenship, Earl Conley and Herman Johns all made attempts to run the hotel's restaurant under names like Frank's Lunch Room and the Country Club Tavern. And Martin Mosley had made a run in the 1940s.

HAZEL KIRKPATRICK

Hazel (Wheeler), wife of Toney Jenkins Post Commander Wilbur Kirkpatrick, operated Hazel's Café at 600 Lafayette Street through most of the 1950s. The couple married in 1940, living at 505 Lafayette Street. He was working for Colonel C.C. Earp at the capitol when he joined the U.S. Army in 1943.[348]

Kirkpatrick also was a leader in the Capitol City Lodge No. 9 AF and AM, among the oldest Black lodges in the state. That organization was chartered in 1867 and built a lodge hall on Jefferson Street in 1904, where it met for at least fifty years.[349]

In the baseball scene, Kirkpatrick was a leading hitter for the Mohawks in the 1930s. When pitching legend "Satchel" Paige and the Kansas City Monarchs, champions of the Negro American League, came to town in 1942, Kirkpatrick managed an all-star team of area players from Fulton,

Jefferson City, Moberly, the penitentiary and the St. Louis Giants.[350] As manager of the Eagles baseball club in 1948, he was vocal in the effort to establish a stadium for Lincoln University.[351]

ELIZABETH ROGERS

The University Grill opened in the fall of 1937 at 603 Lafayette Street under Elizabeth (Brown) Rogers, who by the age of seven had baked her first cake and by eighteen was winning county fair prizes for her cooking. She and her sisters operated a restaurant in their hometown of Richmond for several years before Elizabeth and her husband, Alec, relocated to Jefferson City with ninety dollars, one table and secondhand dishes.[352]

The Rogerses quickly outgrew their location and moved to 629 Lafayette Street, where they had seating for twenty-two and could employ three students. Within five years, they required another move to a new brick building, across Dunklin Street, at 630 East Dunklin Street. Here the University Grill could seat forty-four and employ nearly a dozen local women and students.[353]

During World War II rationing, it was sometimes a challenge to prepare quality meals, the Rogerses told the *Clarion* in 1946. Fried chicken was one of Elizabeth's most popular plates. And after the war, the *Clarion* said it was "nothing to find [up to] 130 students waiting for service on a moderately busy day" at the University Grill.[354]

After Elizabeth Rogers died in 1949, Wilbur and Hazel Kirkpatrick briefly operated the grill.[355] By the spring of 1950, Leona Harris had taken over, serving home-cooked food and pies.[356] Then, the next year, Chris G. Griffin was proprietor, with a menu of barbecued meats and plate lunches.[357]

THE TOPS

Perhaps the longest-operating restaurant in the Foot was the Tops at 626 Lafayette Street.

Martin Moseley opened a restaurant at 626 Lafayette Street, his home, as early as 1925. Before Moseley, it had been a private residence dating back to 1908. During Prohibition, it was the site of at least one liquor raid, when

```
Glover's DeLuxe Barbecue
PREPARED FRESH DAILY AT
THE TOPS
BEVERAGES          SANDWICHES
Lafayette at Dunklin                    Phone 3646
```

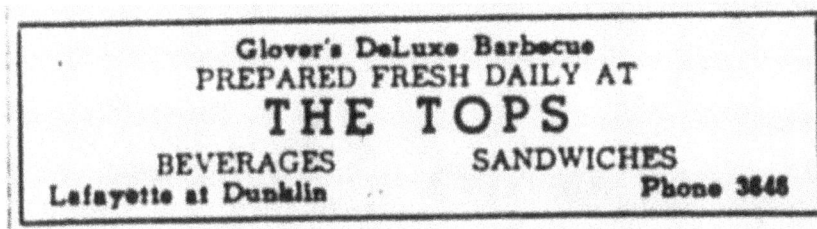

Advertising in the 1947 *Lincoln Clarion* for the Tops Restaurant and Glover Brown's "deluxe" barbecue. *Photo courtesy of Lincoln University Archives.*

Ella Mosely and Fred Foster were arrested for having a small amount of whiskey, 14 quarts of beer and 108 quarts of home brew.[358]

The University Barber Shop operated in the restaurant's basement from 1933 to 1959.

Wilbur Brown started the Tops Barbecue in 1941 at 626 Lafayette Street, which also was his home. In 1947, new owner Glover Winfrey Brown Sr. built a new facility on the lot, with seating for seventy, a thirty-foot bar and the latest kitchen appliances in the same location.[359]

"I believe in putting back into the business a large part of the profits earned and the only way to do that is to give the people bigger and better entertainment values," Brown said.[360]

In 1949, the Tops added a sidewalk café with tables and chairs in front, for passersby to stop for a cool beverage. At the same time, a pavilion was added to the back, extending to Weir's Creek.[361]

Brown also added a jukebox, playing one hundred selections vertically, in the spring of 1949. "Mr. Brown is well-known around these parts for always doing improvements on his tavern," the 1949 *Clarion* reported.[362]

Glover Brown Sr. was born in Blackwater and moved to Jefferson City in 1929.[363] As early as 1934, Brown operated a soft drink place and restaurant at 517 Linn Street, formerly the Donaldson Clark restaurant, just across the street from his home at 522 Linn Street.[364]

With an eighth-grade education, Brown worked his way up from janitor to state employee to owning his own business. In the 1940s, the Lincoln business program held an annual conference on job prospects for future graduates. For several years, Brown was invited as part of a professional panel discussing "Starting a Business on Your Own."[365]

The "special sauce" Brown topped his barbecued burgers with was almost as popular with students and locals as his wife, Bertha (Webb), who took care of the money and day-to-day operations at the Tops.[366]

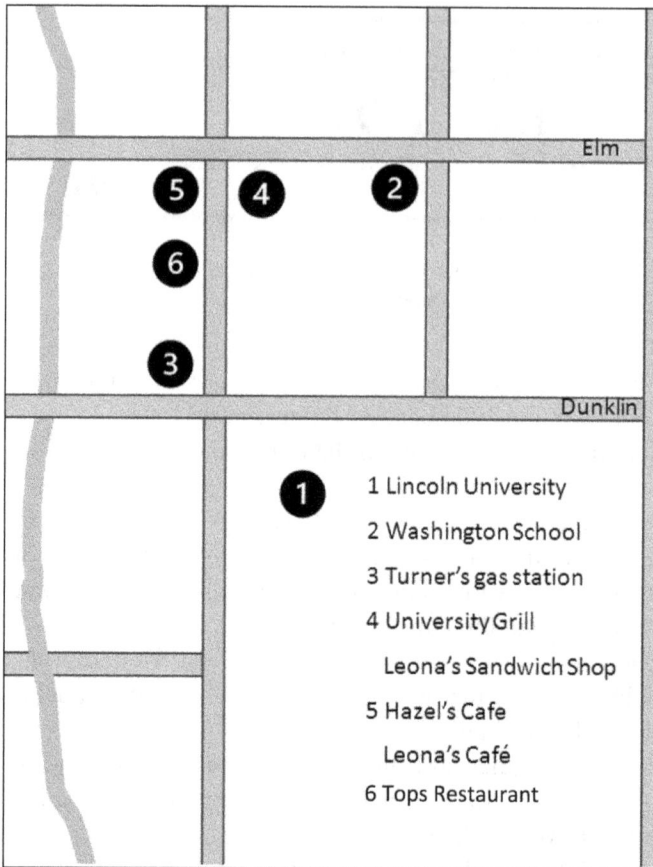

1 Lincoln University

2 Washington School

3 Turner's gas station

4 University Grill

Leona's Sandwich Shop

5 Hazel's Cafe

Leona's Café

6 Tops Restaurant

Map of memorable restaurants in the Foot. *Map by Michelle and Stephen Brooks.*

Bertha also took care of the Lincoln students with curfews—girls 9:00 p.m. and boys 10:00 p.m.—by delivering burgers, hot dogs and cold sodas to the dorms between 10:00 p.m. and midnight.[367] Even if the students couldn't pay right away, they could get a meal ticket or work off the cost.[368]

Missouri governors appreciated the Tops' food, too. Governor James T. Blair would be chauffeured to the Tops' rear door. And Governor Warren Hearns had Bertha Brown cater a birthday with barbecued raccoon, which started a wild game day tradition.[369]

Traveling teams and their following crowds would stop at the Tops before or after their games with Lincoln University.[370]

Don Webb remembers working from a young age at his stepfather's business, serving tables, washing dishes, cleaning floors or whatever else needed doing. Behind the businesses and neighborhood homes, Webb and many from the neighborhood learned to play ball. They also swam in Weir's Creek before the Community Pool opened in 1949 (it closed in 1975).[371]

His barbecue's popularity came from Brown's "special sauce" recipe and the fact that he would both marinate the meat with it, then top it, Don Webb remembered.[372] The flavor was so memorable that Hunt's Foods approached Brown Sr. about franchising.[373]

Glover Brown Jr. said his father's nemesis was Ollie Gates of Gates BBQ in Kansas City. The elder Brown would joke, "You know how they make their barbecue sauce, don't you?...Them old Maytag washing machines, that's what Ollie Gates makes his barbecue sauce in."[374]

The family story goes that Ollie Gates' father ate the barbecue at the Tops and then opened his own open pit barbecue place at the corner of Prospect and Sutton in Kansas City, Arthur Brown said. "He tried his best to get my dad to tell him what was in his BBQ sauce," Arthur Brown recalled.[375]

"That's kind of what made our family stand out, because everybody knew that the Tops was the trendy place to be in the black community because of all the celebrities would come here because of the barbecue," Glover Brown Jr. said.[376]

PART III

LOST CEMETERIES

Chapter 11

INTRODUCTION

The earliest-known burials in what is today Jefferson City were made nearly a millennium ago by people of the Mississippian Neolithic culture. Several of their distinctive burial mounds dotted the southern ridge overlooking the Missouri River.

In particular, burial mounds were removed from the present capitol grounds, the Richmond Hill overlook and at the Ike Skelton Missouri National Guard training site.

The writer of Goodspeed Publishing Company's *History of Cole County* (1888) said, "A few more years and they will have disappeared under the ravages of progress, and for thousands of years the world will look in vain for actual testimonials of a people who were here before us. Preserve these precious monuments of an age gone by, so that those who are to come will not charge the present with vandalism and ignorance."

Unlike these ancient burials, whose names and customs are lost to time, several younger burial grounds in the city have been relocated with efforts to record names, if not retain headstones.

The city's oldest modern cemetery is Old City Cemetery, at the corner McCarty and Chestnut Streets. It is distinguished from the adjacent Woodland Cemetery by the orientation of the headstones. In the mid-1800s, the "Christian tradition was to inter the dead with their feet facing east…in anticipation of the second coming of Christ," said cemetery preservationist Nancy Thompson.

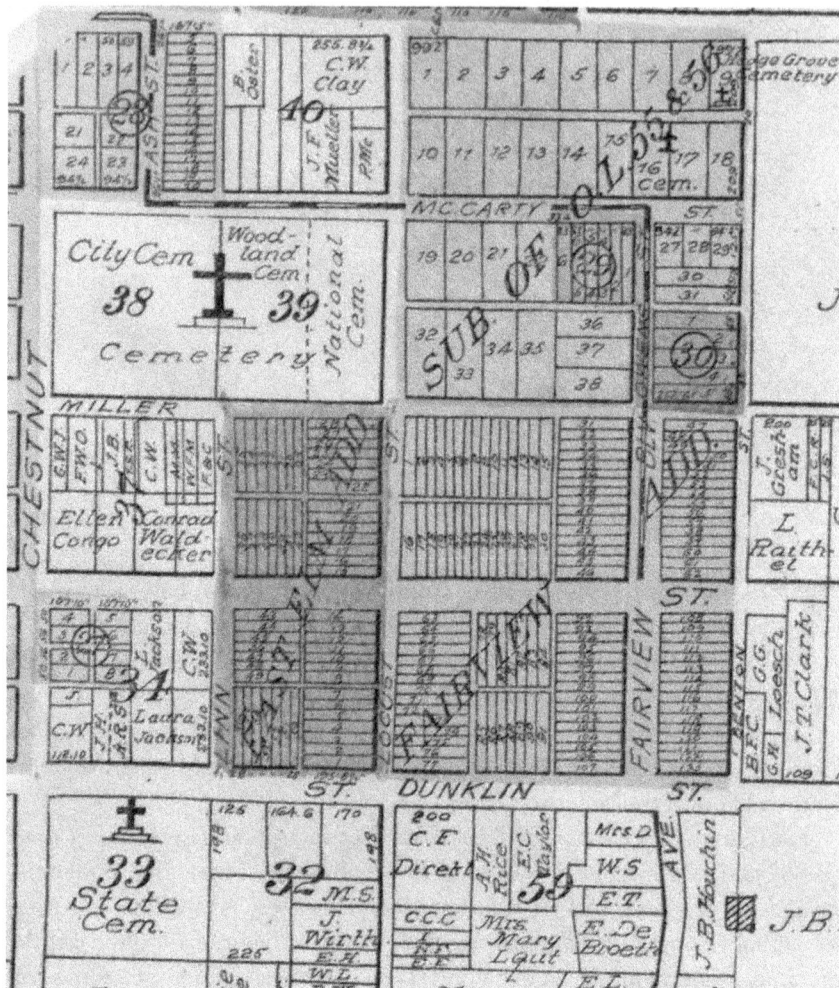

This map by the Sanborn Fire Insurance Company shows State Cemetery, Hedge Grove and Maple Grove. *Photo from Library of Congress.*

In following years, smaller, private cemeteries opened, including St. Peter's #1, Hedge Grove, Maple Grove and one kept by the state. All of these, whether by progress or by time, are no longer. The place where mourners said goodbye is gone, but the headstones and some remains were relocated.

Before the dead were put in the ground in the nineteenth century, they were prepared and visited in the home. Windows, doorknobs, mantels and picture frames were covered with black fabric called crepe.

"Funerals in the 1800s were a very public affair....The body was laid on display in a coffin in the parlor of the home. As news spread throughout the town, people would stop to view the body and bring food for the family," according to Mississippi's Manship House Museum.

Many superstitions surrounded this process. Mirrors were covered, because the belief was that the next person to see the reflection of the deceased would also die. Clocks were stopped to avoid bad luck. And bodies were carried out feet first, so the deceased could not "look back at the house and beckon others to join them in death," according to Hoag Levins of Historic Camden County, New Jersey.

The gift of flowers aided in covering the smell. Embalming became more common in the United States during the Civil War. Afterward, furniture stores, which had provided wooden caskets, began taking on the business of undertaking, and eventually funeral services moved from homes to designated funeral parlors.

The city's first public funeral home was opened about 1929 at the Victorian-style 712 East High Street by the sons of German immigrant furniture makers Jacob Heinrichs and Gerhard Crevelt.

Heinrichs added funeral services to his furniture business in 1861. His son John studied at the business college of Wyman University in St. Louis and took over the business operations in 1879. The year before, his father had taken over the business of Stampfli & Vaughan, located on the main floor of Bragg Hall, 234 East High Street. By 1900, the business was located at 205–207 East Main Street and had three undertakers.

Today's burials are remembered with well-kept, large cemeteries, published obituaries and Internet-based memorials.

Chapter 12

MAPLE GROVE

The death of one of the earliest Jewish settlers of Jefferson City spurred the formation of the Jefferson City Hebrew Cemetery Association, which established the Maple Grove Cemetery in 1879 in the 1300 block of East McCarty Street.[377] Before that, early Jewish settlers in Jefferson City were taken to St. Louis for proper burial.

Moritz, Louis, Simon and Joseph Obermayer opened a successful mercantile in uptown Jefferson City while also making their own caps.[378] Moritz Obermayer emigrated from Bavaria in 1844, and his brothers later followed. Together, they operated one of the longest-running uptown stores in the nineteenth century, Obermayer & Brothers.

When Moritz Obermayer died in 1876, his funeral was one of the largest ever witnessed in the city. The Masonic fraternity carried his remains from his home to the train station, where it was taken for interment in the St. Louis New Mt. Sinai Cemetery.[379]

The association also organized the Congregation Beth El, meaning House of God, to promote the reform Jewish faith in the Capital City. The synagogue, designed by local architect Frank B. Miller and funded by the Hebrew Ladies Sewing Society, followed in 1883.[380]

The first interment at Maple Grove was in 1879 for the accidental death of cigar maker William Rose. Born near Berlin in 1822, he immigrated to Moniteau County by 1867, when he married Ernestine, who was later buried beside him. He opened a tobacco store in California, Missouri, in 1870 and moved it to High Street in Jefferson City by 1873.

The Goldman family represented nearly one-third of burials relocated from Maple Grove Cemetery to the Jewish section of Riverview Cemetery. *Photo courtesy of Nancy Arnold Thompson.*

Several of the twenty-nine burials at Maple Grove Cemetery were for children of congregation members.[381]

Abram Straus, born in 1800, was the oldest to be buried at Maple Grove in 1889. He was the father of original congregation organizers Joseph and Jacob, who operated the Strauss Saddlery Company inside the Missouri State Penitentiary.[382]

Jacob Strauss & Co. had opened by 1869 in St. Louis.[383] Like many businessmen taking advantage of the inmate labor of the time, Jacob Strauss & Co. moved to Jefferson City by 1875, when it was making forty horse collars per day with 125 men.[384] At that time, three other businesses within the walls made shoes and the J.S. Sullivan Co. was making saddle trees.

It was in the Strauss shop that the riot and fire attributed to John "Firebug" Johnson started in 1883. The shop used rye for its collars, which easily was set alight by convict Dave Taylor. The inmates cut the fire department's hose as it attempted to put out the blaze. The fire destroyed all of Strauss' harness, collar and whip factories, as well as the nearby shops of Giesecke Boot and Shoe, Misenburg's Shoe, State Weaving, State Machine and Excelsior Loom.[385]

Nearly one-third of the Maple Grove burials were for the Goldman family, including Minnie (Lavotoch) who was among the Hebrew Ladies Sewing Society organizers, and Jacob, who was one of the first trustees for both the congregation and the cemetery.[386]

Jacob Goldman emigrated from Prussia at age sixteen with his brother, Joseph, in 1859. They arrived in Jefferson City by 1870 and opened a store, Jacob Goldman & Bro. Later, the business at 211 East High Street was operated by Jacob and his sons, Samuel and Mendell, who partnered with Paul Kaiser after their father's retirement. Of Jacob Goldman's thirteen children with his wife, Mina, six were buried at Maple Grove, as well as a granddaughter. Another son and a daughter-in-law were later buried with the family at Riverview, after the relocation.

Another of the congregation's first trustees who is buried at Maple Grove was Abraham Heim. He was a popular clothier.[387] Like Goldman, Heim immigrated as a teenager, but his home was Bavaria. Heim gained experience as a clothing salesman in Ohio before arriving in Jefferson City in 1870. He worked for Sachs & Wolferman and then operated his own store inside the City Hotel from 1873 to 1883, when he bought his own storefront at 134 East High Street. Called "Colonel Heim" by his friends, he retired in 1905, selling to his longtime clerk, Lafe Bacon.[388]

Other surnames from Maple Grove included Baer, Czarlinsky, Drukker, Goldberg, Gross, Hochstadter, Novak, Rauh, Schiele and Vetsburg.

Eminent domain for road construction claimed Maple Grove Cemetery.[389] Julius Meyerhardt gained permission from family members of the interred and negotiated the removal of twenty-seven bodies to a dedicated section in Riverview Cemetery in 1932.[390]

Chapter 13

HEDGE GROVE

E arly African American burials were interred at the west end of Old City Cemetery. There, hundreds of men and women lie today without headstones, which likely had been fieldstones or wooden markers lost to time.

Later, a "colored burying ground" at the southwest corner of Dunklin and Chestnut Streets was used, before 1877. The troublesome spot was more rock than soil, and the site was so full, graves held two coffins.[391]

Black residents in 1877 organized the private Hedge Grove Cemetery Association. The new lot was at the east end of High Street when they bought it; the cross street of Benton was cut through later.[392]

The organizers of the new Black cemetery asked for city aid to fence in the burial ground because the former location, now on the Lincoln campus, was "nothing more than the commons, over which the stock roam."[393]

Among those appointed from the Black community to see this project through were respected leaders Archie Drake and Howard Barnes.[394]

Born in Virginia, Drake came to Missouri with the Patterson family and was enslaved by J. Christopher Watson in Cole County before he enlisted at Jefferson City. Although he was rejected before being mustered in to the Sixty-Seventh U.S. Colored Troops at Benton Barracks in St. Louis, he still gained his freedom.[395]

After the war, Drake amassed considerable property southeast of the city limits, which eventually became valuable as the city grew. His property included a dairy in the 1000 block of East Dunklin Street, which was the end of the street at the time, and five acres, which his stepdaughter leased to the Milton Hospital for African Americans after his death in 1907.[396]

In the early days of Lincoln Institute, Drake operated a boardinghouse and kitchen. He was an early deacon of Second Baptist Church and a charter member of the Capital City Lodge No. 9 AF and AM.[397]

Drake also was involved in Republican politics, running for Jefferson City postmaster, serving as butler in the Executive Mansion for Governor B. Gratz Brown and Governor Thomas Crittenden and being elected several times as a convention delegate. Floyd Shoemaker wrote in 1945 for the State Historic Society of Missouri of a governor's ball for Brown, when Drake greeted guests at the door "resplendent in evening clothes." Because both Brown and Drake had "long flowing whiskers," one new legislator said to Drake, "Ah, Governor, delighted to see you looking so well."[398]

Barnes was a state-renowned cook and caterer, operating kitchens in downtown restaurants and hotels, including City Hotel and the Delmonico, as well as his own hotel. He purchased his freedom and his family's after serving as a wagon train cook. He was enslaved at the time by Thomas Jefferson Boggs, brother to Governor Lilburn Boggs, who was part of a Howard County troupe to California during the 1849 gold rush.

Barnes' restaurant "was the resort of all the prominent public men who visited the capital during and between sessions of legislature.[399] He knew them all and can relate interesting anecdotes of peculiarities and characteristics of some of Missouri's early-day statesmen and politicians....Many have been the political conferences and the making and breaking of political slates over the venison steaks and other culinary delicacies with which Uncle Howard tempted his patrons."[400]

By the end of the Civil War, Barnes was financially and socially successful. In the early years of Lincoln Institute, he served as a trustee and used his own property as collateral for the school to qualify for a loan to build its first building on the hilltop campus. And when Lincoln's existence was threatened, Barnes persuaded local lawyer J.E. Belch to run for the state legislature and put through a bill to rescue the school.[401] Barnes-Krekel Hall, demolished in the 1960s on the Lincoln campus, was named for him and white federal judge Arnold Krekel, another early trustee.[402]

Also active in Republican politics, Barnes was the first African American on the city ballot, as the 1874 candidate for mayor, and also the first on a statewide ballot, as candidate for railroad commissioner, in 1880. In 1882, he was elected treasurer of the National Colored Men's Convention, under J. Milton Turner as president.

Like Drake, he was a charter member of the 1866-organized Capital City Lodge No. 9 AF and AM and an early trustee at Second Baptist Church.[403] By the 1880s, Barnes had accumulated quite a fortune, and his family lived in a substantial brick home on West Main Street near the capitol.[404] Barnes and his sons were instrumental in securing land for Hedge Grove.

During its thirty-eight-year activity, Hedge Grove received fifty-one known burials. The first could have been Mary A. Brown, cemetery preservationist Nancy Thompson said. Brown was twenty-three when she died in 1864, more than a decade before Hedge Grove opened. It is likely she was moved, like many, from the old Black cemetery, which was behind the state's burial ground for Missouri State Penitentiary inmates at Dunklin and Chestnut Streets, where the water feature in front of Page Library is today.[405]

"The land was essentially flat with a low rock wall behind it that suggested former use as a quarry," South Side historian Walter Schroeder recalled of the old state cemetery.[406]

The General Assembly had appointed a sexton and provided appropriations for maintenance from 1874 forward for the Dunklin Street cemetery. Remaining burials at this cemetery for inmates and African Americans were relocated in the 1930s by Vic Buescher of Buescher Funeral Home to the city's Longview Cemetery, which opened in 1925 at 204 Scotts Station Road.[407]

The burials at Hedge Grove also were eventually moved to the city's Longview Cemetery.

Hedge Grove Cemetery served from 1878 to 1916. Of the fifty-one known burials at Hedge Grove, the last was newborn Henry E. Anthony, son of Elmore, who shares a grave with his mother, Mary.[408]

The cemetery association's trustees and heirs died or moved away. By 1931, few knew of Hedge Grove's existence on the high bank of Benton and High Streets.[409]

The land was sold by Cole County sheriff L.A. Snorgrass at public auction in 1934.[410] G.W. Dupee was the only surviving trustee of the Hedge Grove Cemetery Association, and he could not pay contractor Louis Brunner after a circuit court ruling required the association to reimburse him $1,300 for street work near the cemetery.[411]

Brunner built Benton Street in the late 1920s. The cemetery association had been unable to pay taxes, and Brunner acquired the property. In 1933, the contractor asked the city to buy the property, since no one bought it at the public sale.[412]

Mary Stokes was known statewide as the cook at the McCarty House. *Sketch from the* St. Louis Republic, *April 28, 1901.*

In 1936, the burials at Hedge Grove were relocated to Longview. However, it was a burden on the Black community, which collected $200 and moved about half of the bodies themselves. Duke Diggs, a distinguished businessman and community leader, received a positive response after asking the city council for help moving the remaining burials.[413]

One of the last burials in Hedge Grove Cemetery was for Mary Stokes. She worked in the kitchen at the McCarty House on McCarty Street from age seven as an enslaved person and through 1906 as a free employee. Stokes worked under Virginia cook Cassandra Crump, who demanded perfect southern cooking. Stokes spent seven years as Crump's assistant before taking over in 1876 as the second of only two head cooks in the hotel's seventy-year history.

Stokes, called "Aunt Mary," carried on her mentor's reputation of southern comfort food, including hot biscuits for breakfast and cornbread for dinner. During the 1904 Democratic convention held in Jefferson City, four newspapermen sent for meals from the McCarty House kitchen. So surprised at their meal, they later visited the hotel, and each gave Stokes a silver dollar as a tip of appreciation for her skill in the kitchen.[414]

At her death, Stokes owned a home in the 400 block of McCarty Street, shares in the Missouri Central Building and Loan Association and an endowment from the Sir Knights and Daughters of Gertrude Adams.[415]

Stokes' son, Robert Wyatt, bought the Silver Moon Hotel and Cafe, with experience from growing up at the McCarty House. He lived at the hotel, 209 Monroe Street, as an employee before becoming the owner, with his wife, Emily. The Silver Moon Hotel was operated first by Gabriel Nash and then Nora Evans.[416]

Wyatt and Emily Stokes rehabilitated the property in 1929, renaming it the New Moon Hotel and serving only white customers. "Few colored people have the courage and confidence to tackle an undertaking like Mr. and Mrs. R.W. Stokes have," the *Jefferson City Post-Tribune* reported.[417] The main floor had two dining rooms plus a lunchroom, which included a barbecue pit. The second and third floors held twenty furnished rooms with closets, as well as a private dining room on the second floor.

Six years later, Emily Stokes was nearly killed when former owner Gabriel Nash fired a pistol through a door, attempting to kill Wyatt Stokes. Nash, eighty and not in his right mind, then committed suicide.[418] Emily and Wyatt Stokes had been caring for Nash and his debts for the last several months at the hotel.

"The Stokes are among the best-known and most highly-regarded Negroes in the community. Their New Moon restaurant is frequented by white people. The Cole County Medical Association had been holding their meetings there for years. A number of elderly white men made their home in the hotel, which enjoyed an excellent reputation," the newspaper reported.[419]

Chapter 14

EVANGELICAL

German Protestants were buried at the same cemetery beginning in 1852. Before that, some were buried in the Old City Cemetery and others on family farms. A difference in denominational views split not only the congregation but also the cemetery.

The early German Protestants met in homes until 1859, when a church constitution was written. In Germany, their religion was called Evangelical Lutheran. But this early gathering of German Protestants soon showed there were distinct differences.[420]

After the Reverend Joseph Rieger arrived in 1860, the Evangelical side, which was more welcoming of all comers, was firmly established at the church on the hill at Washington and Ashley Streets.[421]

The more traditional Lutherans "held rigidly to the unaltered Augsburg Confession and Luther's Catechism," the church's history explained. Eventually, the Lutherans began meeting in homes again, until 1869, when Trinity Evangelical Lutheran Congregation was formed.[422]

In 1871, the German Evangelical congregation voted to strike out names of charter members who now were among the Lutheran congregation. At the same time, the Lutheran trustees initiated a lawsuit to determine ownership of the cemetery.[423]

The early cemetery's donor, Adam Routzsong, had designated the site at the south end of Broadway for the use of "Lutherans." Both the Cole County Circuit Court and the Missouri Supreme Court ruled that the Evangelical church could no longer use that cemetery.[424]

The German Evangelical congregation bought a piece of land from George Wagner, three blocks from the church, on the south end of Washington Street, west along Broadway and just north of the Lutheran cemetery. A fifteen-foot-wide strip of land to Fillmore Street provided access to the cemetery.

The new cemetery was called Gemeinde Friedhoff; in English, the Congregational Cemetery. Men of the church hand-built a sturdy stone-arch bridge across a ravine at the Washington Street entrance in 1890, and a gate was added in 1891.[425]

Lots in the cemetery were sold to members in 1877, the first purchases going to three widows. Among them was Henriette Rieger, widow of the first pastor. Reverend Rieger and other Evangelical members were reinterred from the Lutheran cemetery to the Evangelical.

Rieger was remembered as pious, sincere, kindhearted and indefatigable in his Christian work. During the Civil War, he accepted the additional duties of chaplain of the Missouri State Penitentiary. And the parsonage, also lost to time, housed the sick and wounded during the war. At his death, Rieger had been a member of the Lincoln Institute Board of Trustees.[426]

Church records reflect thirty-two burials recorded from 1871 to 1875, before the church acquired the cemetery. Nearly all of the lots in the Congregational Cemetery had been purchased, though many were yet vacant, by 1911, when Riverview Cemetery opened.[427]

Committees from the church kept the cemetery in good care, paid for by memorial gifts. Many family plots had their own fences.[428]

"It was a secluded, restful, shaded haven in a valley and overflowing with violets, lilies of the valley, euonymus and ivy," the church history said.[429] "Members once fenced and cared for it, dug the graves themselves and lowered caskets into them, decorated graves, and prayed at them."[430]

When the Panorama Hills subdivision was developed in 1939, a new main entrance from the extended Broadway was installed.[431]

The last burial in the Evangelical Cemetery was for William H. Wagner in 1962.[432]

By the time of the cemetery's relocation, South Elementary School bordered the secluded setting to the south, and homes were built up around the burial ground on the other three sides. It was surrounded by a rusted, woven wire fence and filled with mature sycamore and elm trees.[433]

Like many of the stereotypical early cemeteries, it was "calm, serene, almost frighteningly peaceful," George Walz wrote in 1965.[434]

The Missouri State Highway Department identified the cemetery location as early as 1956 to be part of the U.S. 54 relocation south of the

Men from the Central Evangelical Church, now Central United Church of Christ, built this stone bridge by hand for access to the early Evangelical Cemetery. *Photo courtesy of Susan Ferber.*

new Missouri River Bridge. Although the construction project required only half of the cemetery property, the highway department agreed to buy the entire area.[435]

The property including the stone-arch bridge was not used in the highway development, and what local historian Gary Kremer calls a "real jewel" still stands—despite minor damage from flaming fuel from the tanker explosion on Missouri 54 in 2007.[436]

"It may be one of the last remaining examples of self-standing stonemasonry of the nineteenth century in Jefferson City…[and] is an excellent example of local craftmanship and labor that built our city in pre-mechanical times," South Side historian Walter Schroeder said.[437]

The 360 graves were relocated to a special Evangelical Section of Riverview Cemetery, large enough to accommodate 560 burials. Member Louis Burkel attempted to gain owner or descendant permission for each of the removals. For those who did not consent or who could not be located, the Cole County Circuit Court issued permission for the relocation.[438]

The removal project was challenging, as church records were not complete, aged remains were difficult to identify and some plots had multiple burials. With the aid of Freeman Mortuary, these burials were reinterred similarly to how they had been at the Congregational Cemetery.[439]

The old tombstones, many with Bible passages inscribed in German, were installed in 1965, in the same order at Riverview as they had been at Evangelical Cemetery, by Freeman Mortuary. [440] The grave markers were dedicated in 1975.[441]

The section at Riverview Cemetery carries the name "Congregational Cemetery," even though the church by then had changed its name to Central United Church of Christ.[442]

Chapter 15

VERY FIRST ST. PETER

M any may be surprised to learn where the first Catholic cemetery in Jefferson City was consecrated: the northeast corner of Bolivar and West McCarty Streets.[443]

Within walking distance of the first St. Peter Church, built of logs by church members, the cemetery served mostly German and Irish immigrants.[444] Reverend Urs Joseph Meister, pastor of the congregation, bought the land on April 15, 1850, for fifty dollars from Andrew and Margaret Hunter.[445]

Those earliest burials are thought to have been reinterred at the second St. Peter's Cemetery on the north side of West Main Street near the present water tower.[446] However, no burial records survived from that earliest burial ground.[447]

In consequence, the stately St. Peter Cemetery, fronted by a green iron fence farther west in the 1200 block of West Main Street, should be considered St. Peter Cemetery #3, though it is commonly referred to as Cemetery #2, said Alan Lepper, caretaker of Resurrection Cemetery.[448]

As this third cemetery reached capacity, Resurrection Cemetery was established in 1935, on one hundred acres for use by four area Catholic parishes.

The first recorded Catholic burial, signed by Jesuit missionary the Reverend Ferdinand Benoit Marie Guislam Helias d'Huddeghem, was made on September 11, 1838, for Richard O'Connor, who likely was buried in the Old City Cemetery.[449]

This early iron cross is one of the more unique markers at St. Peter's Cemetery. The German inscription is for Franz Joseph Goetz (1798–1869). *Photo courtesy of Nancy Arnold Thompson.*

Many Irishmen were drawn to Jefferson City at this time as builders for the second statehouse. O'Connor probably had been a member of that crew. His burial was followed not long after by fellow Irish Catholic John O'Brien.[450]

Jesuit records said about two hundred Catholics lived in Jefferson City by the fall of 1838. Although Helias visited them from his home church at Westphalia, they had not yet built a church in the Capital City.

The first Catholic Mass celebrated in the Capital City was by the Reverend Felix Verreydt in 1831. Afterward, the parish met in homes and later in the first statehouse building before its fire in 1837.

The Catholics' first permanent building was built of oak logs in 1846, when the mission joined the St. Louis Diocese as a parish.

Cemetery #1 was built four years later, near the neighborhoods of Goose Bottom and Richmond Hill. Within a year of the cemetery opening, the residents had petitioned the city council. The area, being typical for the city, was mostly rock and clay, making the smell and pollution of the decaying bodies offensive.[451]

The church began interring at Cemetery #2, which it purchased in July 1855.[452] Those buried there that first year included four-year-old George Brenneisen and Helen Altgilbers, who was interred twenty-five years before her husband, Herman.[453]

In the mid-1850s, this area was outside the city limits and stood alone in a park-like setting. Today, these burials are hidden behind Heisinger Bluffs, and most of the markers show the damage of weather and vandalism.

Margaret Fitzpatrick may be the oldest person in the plot, having been born in 1794 and buried at age eighty-seven. She and her husband, John, lived a block south of the church on Broadway. And Wendler Gehring, who had been a private in the Tenth Missouri Cavalry, was buried in 1879 with a veteran's marker.

The latest recorded burial in 1885 was Ellen Brannan, wife of Hugh Riley, who had emigrated from Kilkenny, Ireland, and died at age forty-five, not long after moving west from Maryland.[454]

By 1884, Cemetery #2 was full, and St. Peter parishioners organized a cemetery association, which opened the spacious Cemetery #3.[455]

By the 1940s, Cemetery #2 was destabilizing, with bones protruding from the bluff. Many of the stones were removed to ease lawn care.[456] Legend says Reverend Joseph Vogelweid had about a dozen headstones reorganized as a path and altar, later.[457]

As a historic landmark of the early Catholic, mostly German, settlers of the Capital City, most of the gravestone information at Cemetery #2 was recorded in 1977 by the Mid-Missouri Genealogical Society.[458]

What markers remain hold familiar local family surnames: Borgmeyer, Crevelt, Fischer, Heinrichs, Hentges, Hough, Kolkmeyer, Kroeger, Moeller, Rackers, Rodeman, Schrimpf, Schulte, Stampfli, Tillman, Upschulte, Wallendorf and Wolters.[459]

Recently, volunteers have been restoring broken markers and identifying burial plots without headstones to preserve the history inside this cemetery for future generations.

PART IV

LOST RECREATION

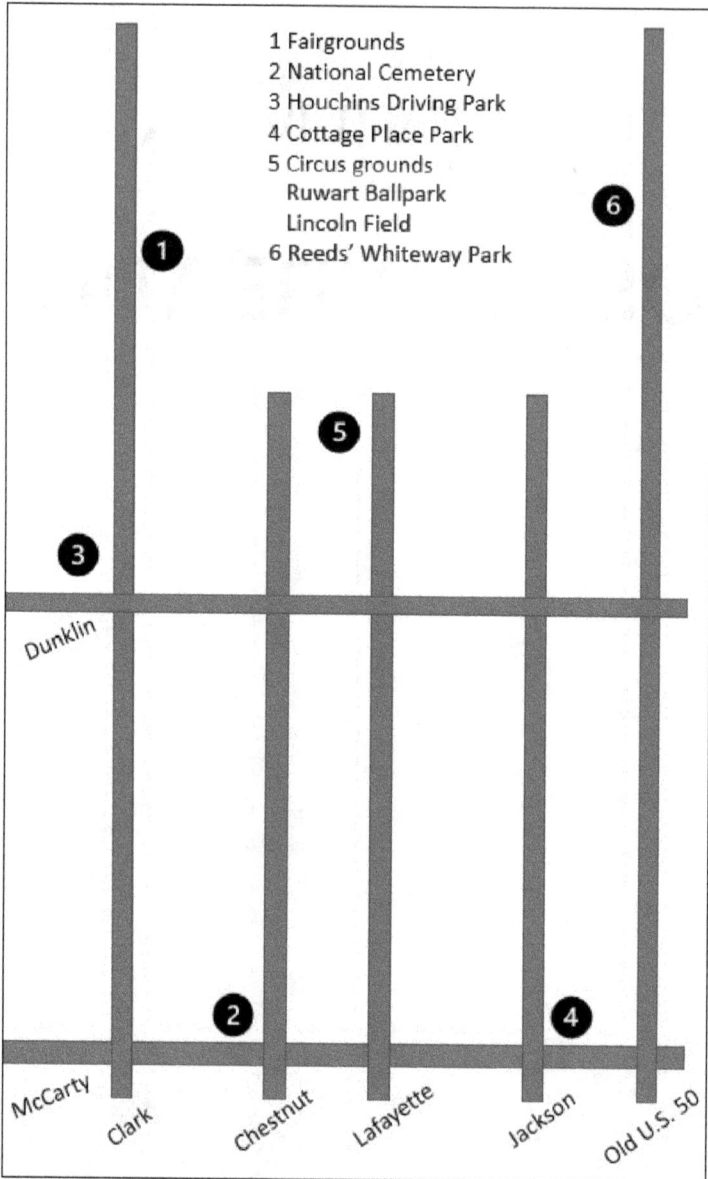

1 Fairgrounds
2 National Cemetery
3 Houchins Driving Park
4 Cottage Place Park
5 Circus grounds
   Ruwart Ballpark
   Lincoln Field
6 Reeds' Whiteway Park

Dunklin

McCarty

Clark

Chestnut

Lafayette

Jackson

Old U.S. 50

Map of lost recreation areas. *Map by Michelle and Stephen Brooks.*

Chapter 16

FIRST FAIRGROUNDS

The Cole County Fairgrounds, before the Civil War, were southeast of the city limits; what today is the tree-lined Wagner subdivision was once the site of community picnics, Independence Day and Emancipation Day celebrations and horse racing.

During the war, the Union troops occupied the site for a time, causing quite a bit of damage. They skirmished with Confederate troops near the fairgrounds, which is the closest the Capital City came to being attacked. An anonymous, self-described "Missouri ex-rebel" recalled, "near the fair grounds, a slight skirmish occurred resulting in but little loss on either side."[460]

The site was under the control of the Cole County Agricultural and Mechanical Association. In 1863, the association had to appoint a committee to preserve the fences, buildings and enclosures from destruction.[461] Then the turnout for the 1865 fall fair was poor.[462]

In January 1866, attentions turned from the war to disease. The city board of aldermen procured the long building at the fairgrounds as a smallpox hospital.[463]

In the spring of 1866, improvements began, including the planting of ornamental trees. And in advance of the fair, a "large force" was called in to make "needful repairs and improvements" following the war's end.[464]

Resuming such a substantial event and bringing together those who had opposed one another in armed conflict, the fair proved to be a success.

The *People's Tribune* said it was an "excellent occasion for our farmers to assemble and compare notes and results, but above all, they are at neutral ground, where, for a few days each year, leaving aside for once all their political, religious and private differences, men meet with a view to good fellowship and innocent amusement solely."

The first Cole County Fair was held in 1862 or earlier, as the association planned its seventh fair in 1869.[465] The Missouri River ferry service and the Pacific Railroad annually reduced fares for fairgoers.

The wooden amphitheater had a bandstand in the center, where racing judges observed during horse, mule and human races around the egg-shaped track. The dangerous narrow turn was near the entrance off of Moreau Drive into Wagner Place today.[466]

The fairgrounds also included stables, a baseball field and swings for children.[467] This was also the preferred site for the shooting sports club exhibitions and competitions.

In addition to hot dog and popcorn stands, beer was sold from a keg and "Billy Roesen's soda water was everywhere on hand," recalled longtime resident John Giesecke.[468]

In the mid-nineteenth century, the local fairgrounds was considered the best equipped of any in the state, outside of St. Louis. When Jefferson Davis, president of the Confederacy during the Civil War, visited in September 1875, he stayed at the old governor's mansion, and his Sunday entertainment was a carriage ride by Burr McCarty's livery to visit the Jefferson City National Cemetery and the fairgrounds.[469]

The site also hosted the annual Independence Day celebration, which included dinner, dancing, recitation of the Declaration of Independence and parades. During the 1892 Fourth of July, more than two thousand people attended the event, which included horse races and a balloon ascension.[470] The balloon ascension began at the fairgrounds with a couple of trapeze artists suspended from the balloon as it rose in the air. Once it took flight, spectators in their buggies raced out of the fairgrounds to see where the balloon would land and if the trapezists were unharmed.[471]

Emancipation Day celebrations also were held on the fairgrounds, bringing in African Americans from surrounding counties. The events were scheduled around September 22, when in 1862 President Abraham Lincoln signed the Emancipation Proclamation. In 1894, the event included a parade, baseball games and speeches by Governor William Stone and Mayor Arthur Grimshaw at the fairgrounds, followed by musical and literary performances at the Lohman Opera House.[472]

Organizations and churches held picnics and fundraisers there. And military units, including the Tenth Missouri Cavalry and the James A. Garfield Grand Army of the Republic Post, hosted reunions.[473]

Problems plagued the site. Being so far out of town was a concern, during a time when most people arrived by foot or carriage. The east side had not developed much past the National Cemetery. John W. Giesecke recalled a zigzag trail from the cemetery south to Green Berry Road, crossing the property of Otis H. Manchester, who was known for his winning pair of light harness buggy mules.[474]

In 1876, residents asked the county court to macadamize—an early form of laying gravel—the road from the city cemetery to the fairgrounds, likely what became Chestnut Street, which was used as a farm-to-market road.[475]

"The fair ground is made a great way off by the bad roads we are compelled to travel to get to it," the *State Journal* reported.[476]

Ferry captain Jefferson T. Rogers, who had served seven times as mayor, turned his efforts toward the fairgrounds following the war, as president of the Cole County Agricultural and Mechanical Association. He "pushed for repair and beautifying of buildings and grounds at the fairgrounds, [including] drives and walks being leveled and graveled."[477]

After Rogers, Gilson Tompkins Ewing, son of Robert and Jane (Ramsey) Ewing, was president of the association for several years until his accidental death falling from a horse in 1876.[478] At the time, he owned the largest farm in the county.

A portion of the Cole County Agricultural and Mechanical Association's land was sold to the state before 1870. The state then transferred what became State Park to the city in the 1940s; it became McClung Park, named for Warden Dickerson Clark McClung. Association members who were property owners in the beginning included Jefferson T. Rogers and his wife, Kizzia; Thomas Lawson Price and wife Caroline; Christopher Wagner and wife Elizabeth; Green Berry and wife Virginia; Gilson Ewing and Eliza; C.F. Lohman and Henrietta; Frederick Rauschelback and Rosalia; John Schott and Henrietta and John Bauer and Barbara.[479]

As early as 1893, the anticipation of a Missouri River bridge provoked the idea of a "magnificent fairgrounds" for Central Missouri on the river's edge in Cedar City, which would host the Cole, Callaway and Boone County fairs.[480]

Then landowner William W. Wagner began planning his subdivision, to replace the fairgrounds, "in order to secure more and better revenue out of it." The most concerned about this prospect at the time may have been the

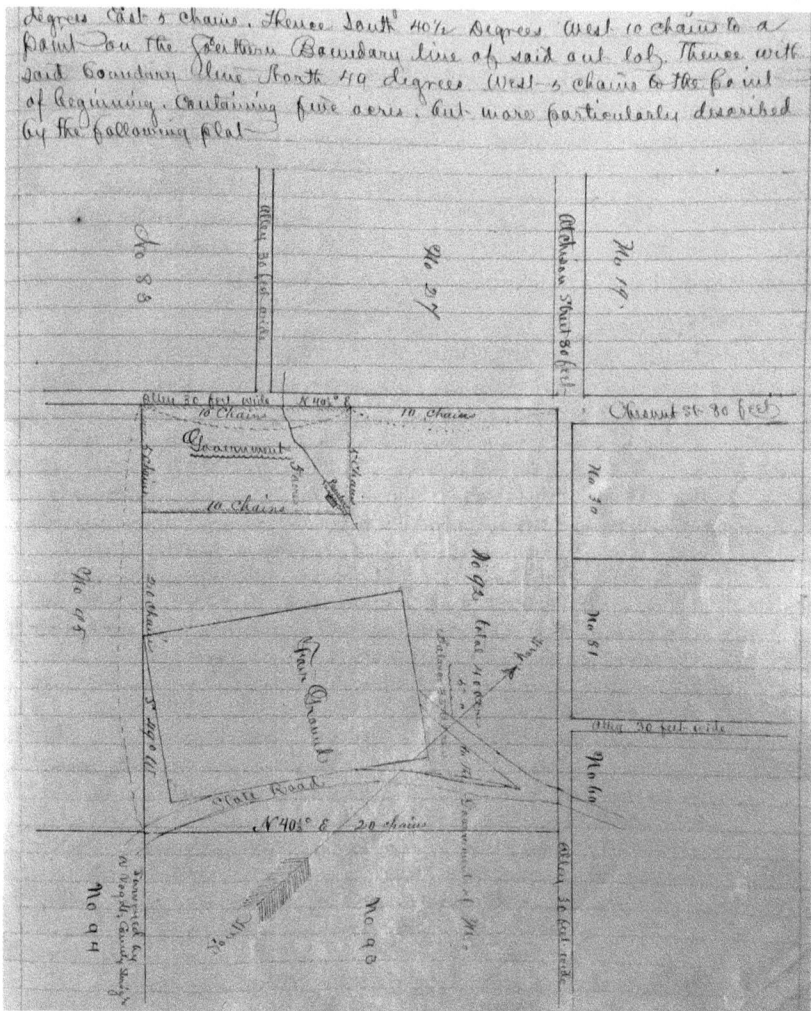

A portion of the Cole County Agricultural and Mechanical Association's land was sold to the state for a park on Chestnut Street, which was transferred to the city in the 1940s, becoming McClung Park. *Cole County Deed Book R, p. 585.*

baseball teams. The sport was a great pastime for players and spectators alike, but it required a significant amount of level ground near the city.[481]

Over time, the site was "permitted to deteriorate and finally collapse and fall into ruin because the will to sustain [the property] wasn't there," the Cole County Historical Society series said.[482] Wagner began improvements for the subdivision that bears his name in 1913.

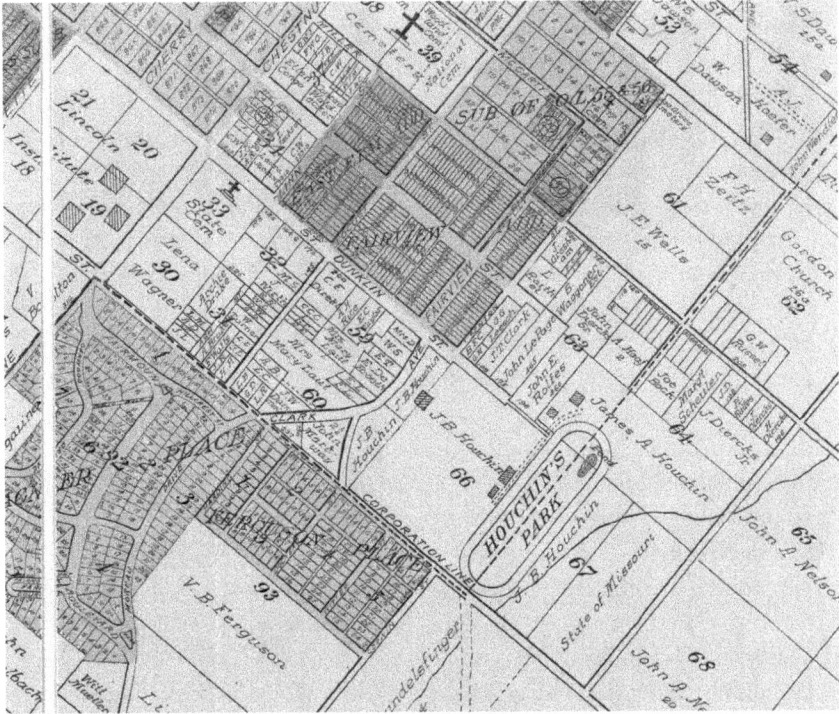

Houchin's Park is at the east end of the developed Dunklin Street in 1914, before McCarty Street has been extended past the cemetery. *Ogle 1914 Plat Map, courtesy of State Historical Society of Missouri.*

But horse racing and the bragging rights to having the fastest horse remained a constant. When one man doubted the speed of another man's horse, they could be found after supper on Capitol Avenue outside the old Madison Hotel. With onlookers gathered along the way, the two would race to Cherry Street and back.[483]

When the old fairgrounds faded, horse racing moved to Houchin's Park, set back from the intersection of Bald Hill Road and Clark Avenue. Houchin's facilities included a half-mile track, likely closer to the level of the Cardinal Street area today, with grandstands and stables to accommodate good-sized shows and races.[484]

Houchin's Driving Park, at 701 Clark Avenue and 1916 Dunklin Street, operated twenty years beginning in 1908, when a newspaper ad lists James Houchin as a breeder of coach, saddle and trotting horses. The horse park became the Bird Haven subdivision in the 1930s.[485] Many state fair winners crossed the finish line at Houchin's Park.[486]

The first saddle stallion from the Houchin stables was Callaway Chief, a consistent winner. But it is Astral King that is the most memorable of these early racers.[487] Astral King was the first horse owned outside of Kentucky to win the Kentucky State Fair Commissioner of Agriculture's Stake in 1915, with rider and trainer L.B. "Splint" Barnett.

Owner James Albert Houchin was born to an Illinois farmer in 1869. He completed business college and moved to Jefferson City in 1891 as the office manager for Charles Lewis Clothing Company, later moving to C.M. Henderson Shoe Company.[488] Houchin in 1895 organized Star Clothing Manufacturing Company, which became one of the largest employers of labor at the Missouri State Penitentiary and grew to fifteen branch factories across the nation.[489]

After retiring from the clothing industry, Houchin became president of the Farmers and Mechanics Bank. Twice he ran for governor, in 1912 and 1916, and he later owned the Monroe Hotel and owned and managed the Madison House.[490]

Houchin had substantial property and stock farms in Cole, Callaway, Morgan and Pettis counties. In 1912, he was elected the first president of the Missouri Saddle Breeders Association.[491]

Houchin's daughter, Myrene, and wife, Mollie (Clark), both were accomplished riders, carrying on the tradition from Mollie's mother, Isabelle Sone Clark, who was "as graceful in the saddle as on the ball floor," former resident Minnie Haughn Boyce recalled.[492]

Chapter 17

COTTAGE PLACE PARK

C ottage Place Park, covering more than a city block at the base of the former Simonsen Ninth Grade Center, or Hobo Hill, was the first intentionally built baseball park in the city.[493] Charles I. Wells sold the undeveloped city block to William W. Wagner in 1888. At the time, the only home in the square was a two-story frame house, occupied by the African American couple George and Susan Vivian (alias Jackson) and their son, who was deaf.[494] George Vivian served with the Sixty-Fifth U.S. Colored Troops, founders of Lincoln University.

A group of businessmen bought the property in 1898 and incorporated as the Cottage Place Realty Company. The public-spirited venture set out to provide public space for various amusements, including baseball games and horse shows. George Hope Sr., a Scottish immigrant tailor, was president, with the board made of shoemen John Tweedie Sr., Henry Priesmeyer and Otis H. Manchester.[495]

The park had been a neighborhood playground; later, it was enclosed with a high board fence, and grandstands were built on the south and west sides. During its use, home plate was laid in three different corners.[496]

Being at the base of Hobo Hill, high school boys could easily watch or wander over to the ball field.[497] Local lore says the name "Hobo Hill" emerged from vagabonds sitting on the slope watching games over the fence top.

In addition to the frequent ball games and horse shows, Cottage Place Park was the stopping point for traveling entertainers, such as Dr. Middleton's

Indian Medicine Show. Once Kearney Speedy held a high-diving exhibition, diving from a sixty-foot platform into a tank of water only three feet deep. And it was commonly known as "Sportsman's Park," since the local gun club made weekly rounds of clay pigeon target practice.[498]

The local baseball team, called the "Jeffs" at one time, was among the best amateur ball teams in the state, winning championships for many years at the turn of the twentieth century. The newspaper's principal sportswriter for the late 1890s was Joe Goldman, who also served Cottage Place Park as official scorer.[499]

The Jeffs hosted big games with traveling professional clubs, including the St. Louis Browns.[500] When the first Missouri River Bridge opened on May 21, 1896, the grand opening and ceremonies on Bolivar Street were followed by other activities throughout town, including a Jeffs versus Browns ball game at Cottage Place Park.[501] James "Tip" O'Neill hit nearly every swing over the left field fence into Lafayette Street.[502] The all-star's nickname "Tip" fell on every young boy with the last name of O'Neill at the time, even longtime U.S. Speaker of the House Thomas "Tip" O'Neill.[503]

Before its end, Cottage Place Park had developed a reputation as "one of the best diamonds in the state," the *Jefferson City Daily Tribune* said.[504]

The baseball field also was used by local horse enthusiasts, who revived the horse show in 1897. The first annual horse show included a variety of exhibitions. But the next year, the focus narrowed when the Jefferson City Horse Show Association organized under outdoorsman Jesse W. Henry as president. Although better organized, the second annual show was hampered by poor weather, though many harness, high-stepping and saddle horses still participated.[505]

The 1900 *Illustrated Sketch Book* described Henry as "a suave gentleman merchant." He came to Jefferson City from Fayette in 1876, when his father was elected a Missouri Supreme Court judge, and the son was awarded the state librarian position.[506]

Henry bought the grocery business of Chris Wagner and William Zuendt, after they were killed in the 1881 train wreck on the Bagnell Branch line to Russellville. He married Kate Madison Davison, daughter of Dr. A.C. Davison. Then, Henry succeeded his father-in-law as president of the First National Bank. He served as treasurer for Central Missouri Trust Company and then cashier at Farmers and Merchants Bank.[507]

In 1895, Henry was appointed the first state game and fish warden. "Perhaps no state in the union has been so liberally endowed with game and fish of the best quality or has been so careless and negligent of

Horse shows were a popular pastime at the turn of the twentieth century, even becoming highly competitive at the regional and state levels. *Photo courtesy of Missouri State Archives, Summers Collection.*

its preservation," the *St. Louis Post-Dispatch* observed. An "expert and indefatigable sportsman," Henry intended to enforce new conservation laws, particularly against dynamiters and to regulate deer and quail hunting.[508]

In its third year, the local horse show association reorganized as the State Horse Show Association of Jefferson City. This time, lawyer and president of Exchange Bank H. Clay Ewing presided. Only George C. Ramsey and L.D. Gordon were held over from the first committee to the next.[509]

As the horse show matured, it shifted attention from mostly Jefferson City horses to a broader market and increased its awards and competition variety.[510] The 1899 program at Cottage Place Park received the attention of the Kansas City *Horse Show Monthly*, which helped bring in big-name competitors like Joe Wheeler, Black Douglass and Bonnie Lassie.[511]

They also introduced a new community tradition: a flower parade in advance of each night's races. Carriages of up to forty vehicles were decorated and drawn through the streets.[512]

In 1900, the fourth year, the committee was led by Judge W.C. Marshall. And the show drew notable participants, including Augustus Busch from St. Louis.[513] Side events included a delivery wagon race, egg and spoon races and a "best gentleman rider" competition.[514]

When the Missouri State Fair started in 1901, the state horse show moved from Jefferson City to Sedalia.[515]

Cottage Place Park served the community well, but it was not a moneymaker. In 1902, Edward Holtschneider bought it from baseball men Harry Sieling and George Stampfli and had it surveyed for building lots.[516] By 1909, former mayor Cecil Thomas and shoe mogul Lester Shepard Parker had bought the park and began selling residential lots as the Parker-Thomas subdivision, ending the career of the city's first intentional ball park.[517]

"It was a beautiful park for a small town and it is a pity that it could not have been held and preserved for a city park. Today, it is only a memory," said George Hope Jr.[518]

Chapter 18

RUWART FIELD

A fter Cottage Place Park sold in the early 1900s, the baseball games found a new home at the old circus grounds in the 900 block of Lafayette Street.[519] Men named Cox and Robinson bought the land in 1909 and converted it to a ball diamond, said to be better than the "old Cottage Place park."[520]

The city's second baseball park was fenced with a grandstand and bleachers. Eventually, the Ruwart brothers—Henry, Jake and William— took over the park, where today's Lincoln University football practice field is.

The Ruwart brothers were born to Henry and Anna (Boeckman). Henry Sr. arrived in St. Louis from Bavaria at age eight. After serving in the Union army, he moved to Jefferson City to work for the J.S. Sullivan Saddletree Company, becoming a partner and eventually superintendent over fifty years.[521]

Henry and Anna built a two-story brick home about 1885 at 731 East High Street, which was one of the first to have indoor plumbing.[522] Eventually, their adult children built homes within a block: Edward at 712 East High Street, Joseph at 210 Cherry Street, William at 214 Cherry Street and Lena Young at 212 Cherry Street.

Anna was instrumental in organizing the Independent Cherry Street Workers, neighbors who joined together to help the less fortunate before the Community Chest or United Way. She was its first president, helping the group buy groceries and clothing for the needy, pay rent for families in distress and provide holiday baskets for low-income families.[523]

In 1905, William, along with brothers Ed and Joe, established their own saddle goods manufacturing company, having learned the business from their father.[524] The Ruwart Manufacturing Company, 105 Monroe Street, eventually added a plant in Denver, Colorado, making horse collars, saddlery, harness and saddle trees.[525]

For a time, the Ruwart Saddlery and Harness Company operated inside the Missouri State Penitentiary.[526] In 1915, the company was making goods for the Studebaker Company and artillery harnesses for the German army, drawing charges from the International United Brotherhood of Leather Workers on Horse Goods that the prison contract was a violation of the nation's neutrality.[527]

After going into receivership, the Jefferson City plant closed in 1926, but the Colorado factory continued through 1936.[528]

The brothers also were distributors for Studebaker, Cadillac and White car manufacturers from about 1919 to 1923.[529] Their shop on Capitol Avenue was "one of the best equipped in Central Missouri."[530] The Ruwart Company also gave longtime mechanic Harry Blackwell his first mechanics job at age seventeen in 1913.[531]

Ruwart Field became a point of real estate controversy in 1921, the same year the first African American Missouri representative took office and the name and role of Lincoln Institute was changed to university.[532]

Lincoln's Board of Regents received a check for $29,500 from the state treasury to purchase two acres of land from Mamie Vineyard and eighteen acres from William Ruwart.[533]

First, the board president, Thomas Speed Mosby, did not have the approval from either the governor or the board to make the requisition from the state auditor's office. Second, immediately after the transaction, Ruwart paid one-third of his proceeds to local banker Howard Cook.[534]

The house committee investigation said, "We come now to the consideration of the well-planned, shameless fraud, by which, with the connivance, if not with the actual participation of certain state officials, Howard Cook through William Ruwart was enabled to obtain from the State Treasury $9,000 without any consideration whatsoever."[535]

Half of the Ruwart eighteen acres was "broken, rocky and unfit for any purpose," the House of Representatives committee report found, though Ruwart had suggested that half could be quarried.[536]

The school's Board of Regents met on December 13, 1920, to discuss a two-year budget to be submitted to the General Assembly. The purchase of land was never discussed, nor added to the 1921–22 budget request. But by

January 6, 1921, Cook had been hired as Ruwart's agent to make a deal. Apparently, Cook assessed the property at $18,000, then fixed the price at $27,000, according to the house committee findings.[537]

Ruwart and President Mosby, who was employed by Cook at Central Trust Company, agreed that Ruwart would sell Lincoln the land for one dollar. Even at this time, the board was not made aware of these steps. And yet, school president Clement Richardson later inserted the $30,000 for land purchase into the budget request.[538]

The idea of Lincoln acquiring the Ruwart property had been casually discussed for some time, so the sudden urgency was never explained. The committee found there was "not the remotest danger of [Ruwart] being able at the time to sell to anyone else."[539]

The house committee, which included Representative Walthall Moore, St. Louis, who introduced the legislation converting Lincoln to university status, declared the situation involved fraud and the knowledge of fraud and deemed the appropriation made by the auditor's office on March 28, 1921, unconstitutional and void.[540]

This was not the first time Jefferson City residents elected to the Lincoln Board of Curators had manipulated the situation for their own benefit. Someone had been making money off of the school's industrial department without compensation to the school. Circulars for a Star Dynamo Company prompted an investigation, which found no such company existed in Jefferson City, yet the dynamo machines had been made by the school's new industrial department and sent south to be sold. According to the *Kansas City Journal*, the dynamos sold for $100 each, but none of the proceeds returned to Lincoln.[541]

After a visit by Governor Arthur Hyde in May 1921, the Lincoln board in early 1922 returned the deed to Ruwart, at the direction of David Peters, special counsel from the state attorney general's office.[542] By 1931, the transaction was completed, making Ruwart's Park the Lincoln Athletic Field.[543]

Ruwart Field already had been used by Lincoln as an athletic field. If the school had not bought the property, the Ruwarts would have platted the land for African American homes, the *Daily Capital News* reported.[544]

William "Biscuit" Ruwart was a pitcher, having played for the St. Mary's College team in St. Mary's, Kansas.[545] He had been "headed for the big leagues until he sustained an injury from which he never recovered sufficiently to regain his old speed."[546]

So, with his brothers, William Ruwart provided the board fence–enclosed site and managed a baseball team, which included Walter Rehg, who later

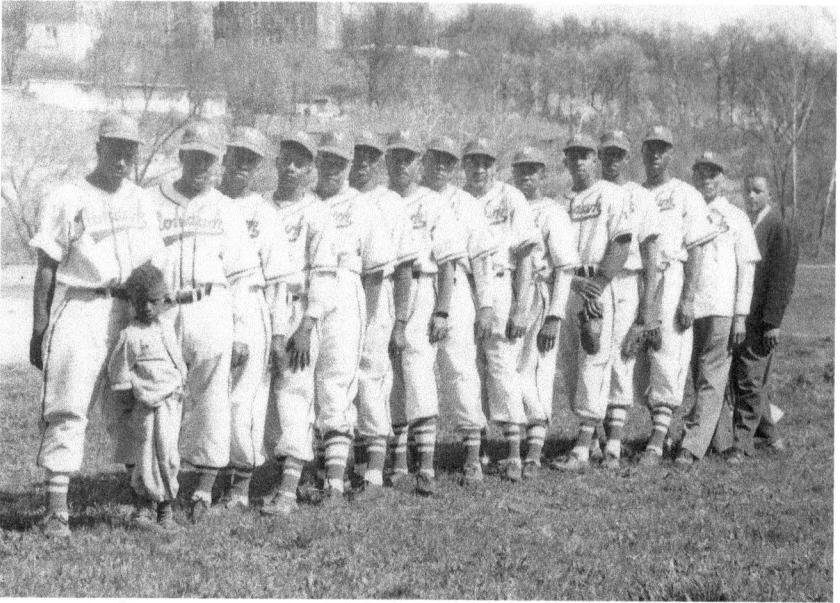

The Jefferson City Mohawks African American baseball team stands on Ruwart Field, later Lincoln Field. *Photo courtesy of Joyce Logan Webb.*

played professionally.[547] William and Jake Ruwart were instrumental in getting a state league organized in 1910.[548] The Missouri League teams were paid and played a schedule of 120 games in Brookfield, Columbia, Kirksville, Macon and Sedalia, as well as Jefferson City.[549]

Ruwart Field was the main stage for the African American teams, drawing from the Foot neighborhood, like the Hubs and the Mohawks. Many professional American Negro Baseball League teams played exhibition games against the local teams at this field in the 1920s. They included the Cuban Stars, the Kansas City Monarchs, the St. Louis Stars and the Birmingham Black Barons.[550] Jefferson City was a convenient and safe stop for the professionals on their way between metropolitan areas.

The Jefferson City Hubs recruited the best African American players from the region, even paying some players to come to town,[551] whereas the Jefferson City Mohawks prioritized local players.

The Mohawks organized in 1922 with the help of Charles "Lefty" Robinson. He was recruited to play full time for the St. Louis Stars, but after one month he quit to make more money working at the capitol and to be closer to his family.[552]

The *Daily Capital News* in 1921 called Robinson "one of the best colored pitchers in the country," when he was playing for the Jefferson City Athletes.[553]

Robinson pitched his first no-run, no-hit game against the Linn team in 1929 and then retired in 1932.[554]

In the community, Robinson was the first modern African American candidate for city office in 1961; the first president of the Jefferson City Community Center, a position he held for fifteen years; the last surviving charter member of the local NAACP branch; and the first Black funeral director.

Chapter 19

WHITEWAY PARK

W hiteway Park was the third and largest of the city's early ball parks, owned by brothers Fred and Joe Reed, who also managed the Jefferson City Senators team.

When Missouri Boulevard was a two-lane Missouri 50, the Reeds plowed and leveled several acres along Heisinger Road for recreation with seating for 3,500 in a grandstand, which included a press box, as well as boxes for chairs.[555]

The ability to play night games was a new amenity in 1930, and the park was as valued to the community as its theaters and capitol tours.[556] The first baseball game at Whiteway Park—named for the appearance of the newly lit road to get there—was in August 1930.[557]

The Reed brothers were born in Livingston County and reared in Fulton, where they both worked in the coal business before moving to Jefferson City, where Joe opened J.D. Reed Coal Company in the Mill Bottom and Fred was a truck driver.[558]

The brothers hoped to revive the champion baseball team reputation of the 1890s Jeffs team.

Fred Reed was manager six years for the Jefferson City Senators semipro team, which played regularly at Whiteway Park.[559] Many of the traveling town teams cherry-picked the best players, no matter where they came from. But the Reeds were known for their policy of giving local talent the first chance.[560]

"Most of all, they want a good ball team. If it can be obtained in Jefferson City, so much the better. If not, they will not hesitate to go elsewhere," the *Jefferson City Post-Tribune* reported.[561]

By the 1931 season, the Senators had a forty-four-game season, and the outfield fence had been moved in to about three hundred feet from home plate.[562] "Ball games without home runs are like gridiron contests without sensational end runs and the managers have decided that something must be done to give the fans more 'thrills,'" the newspaper said.

The park was a welcome distraction for the many families hurting from the effects of the Great Depression. In May 1931, Henry Crevelt Sr. arranged for all gate receipts at home games of the Crevelt Home Furnishers team to be distributed among the players, who were unemployed at the time. Crevelt also arranged single-fee cab rides for a dime, to encourage attendance.[563]

Whiteway Park also welcomed the Jefferson City Mohawks, the local African American team managed by former pitcher Lefty Robinson. The park hosted the Negro Baseball Championships for several years, with the local Mohawks team making a good showing annually. They often faced the St. Louis Pullmans, which dominated the eastern part of the state.[564]

A Capital Softball League took shape in 1933, including several of the statewide elected officials. "The games in this league are bitterly contested and are giving the fans, who have been turning out pretty good, no little amusement, due to the continuous arguing and bitter struggle each team puts up," the *Post-Tribune* reported.

The Reeds organized the Jefferson City Knot-Hole Gang for young baseball fans, who could earn season tickets by working one hour cleaning the park. More than four hundred youths were at the park the first day. Now, these boys "will have a regular seat in the bleachers instead of a hard-earned and none too easily kept position at one of the knotholes in the fence surrounding the park."[565]

The Reeds developed other entertainment to draw as large a crowd as possible. Mohawks manager Lefty Robinson also organized an African American string band and vocal group, which performed often for games at Whiteway.[566]

Perhaps of equal importance to having a place for the locals to play were the exhibitions and traveling events. For example, in September 1930, pitcher Pea Ridge gave a spectacular finish to the ninth inning when his Kansas City Blues played the local team. With a capacity crowd, he sent all but his catcher, Pat Collins, to the bench, playing the inning by himself, the *Post-Tribune* reported.[567]

Another time, the Reeds brought the Kansas City Bloomer Girls to town "at great expense," according to the *Post-Tribune*.[568]

Four St. Louis Cardinal players joined the Jefferson City Senators for a game against the Fulton All-Star team in 1932. They included Paul Derringer, John "Pepper" Martin, Jerome "Dizzy" Dean and Jim Wilson. Derringer and Dean split the pitching, Martin played third base and Wilson was behind the plate. Dean had broken several Cardinals team records that season, and Martin had been the star of the 1931 World Series.[569]

The developing field hosted more than baseball. Attempts were made to organize local football teams, too. In September 1930, the Jefferson City Golden Bears hosted the Warrensburg Mules. But the local team had little experience or bulk. "The Warrensburg style of play, replete with passes, fakes and reverses, completely baffled the Jeffersonians throughout the game," the local paper reported.[570]

The public high school Jays team held its 1930 home opener and its first-ever night football game at Whiteway in October.[571] The Jays continued to play there for several seasons, as did the Jefferson City Junior College Bears and the St. Peter's High School Saints.

In the fall of 1931, Whiteway Park drew large crowds for greyhound racing, called the "Sport of the Gods."[572]

Local organizations held fundraisers and events there, too. Boxing matches, donkey baseball, goose- and turkey-shooting matches, circuses and other outdoor spectacles found the park well-equipped.[573]

To raise money for the milk and ice fund for the city's poor, the Lions Club annually held a Terrapin Derby, with more than 150 entries. Side contests included kittenball and a watermelon-eating contest.[574]

Whiteway also was a popular place for the annual benefit program for the Tuberculosis Society. The "fats" and "leans" were the baseball teams.[575] The event included boys' relay races and a women's golf driving contest, a wrestling match, a sword-swallowing act and a performance by the Schnitzelbankers.[576] Another year, the Modern Woodmen provided a uniformed drill team, and Amos 'n' Andy with their "Fresh Air Taxi Cab" performed for a crowd of two thousand.

Outside of baseball, the largest events at Whiteway Park were likely the horse shows. A grand, three-day horse show was held in May 1931, after the Jefferson City Horse Show Association reorganized again. An important piece of the success of this revival was having James Houchin, who Lawrence Lutkewitte called the "body and soul of all horse activities," on the board of directors.[577]

The Reeds built stables with fifty stalls at the park, and the loudspeaker was improved for announcements. The broadcasting system was loaned to the horse show association, so Captain Heiny from WOS radio could do the announcing.[578]

Polo matches were organized that spring.[579]

Nearly 130 local businessmen contributed more than $4,000 toward the affair.[580] Even the Capital City Telephone Company pitched in, having its operators add, "Don't forget the horse show," when a caller gave their number to be placed.

About one hundred horses were brought into the park, and visitors were invited to look them over during the day.[581] It had been twenty years since a horse show had been held in the Capital City. A parade led by state and city officials was to go downtown, along McCarty and then along Missouri 50 to the park.[582] "The unfamiliar clatter of some high-stepping horses has drawn the eyes of townspeople," the *Daily Capital News* said.[583]

The horse show continued at Whiteway Park through 1934, when more than two thousand spectators filled the grandstands.[584]

Despite the Reed brothers' community-minded developments, they could not control the weather. In the second spring of their park, they had to cancel three events before mid-May. "The Reeds are eagerly awaiting the cry of 'play ball' after several weeks' delay."[585]

In June 1932, a storm with strong wind and hail caused significant damage to the capitol's roof and dome. That storm also ripped up lighting poles at Whiteway Park, mangled the grandstand and blew down two hundred feet of fence. Dressing room windows were broken and a locked door crushed.[586]

A week after the great storm, the Reed brothers sold Whiteway Park to J.W. Miller.[587] A league of six church teams had been playing regularly at the field. One of Miller's first changes was to disband that league, looking to form a city team from the best players of those teams and revive the Jefferson City Senators for competition against out-of-town teams.[588]

"The new management at Whiteway Park is bending every effort to bring high-class baseball back to Jefferson City," the *Post-Tribune* said.[589] Miller also instituted "Ladies Night," where women with escorts or in groups were admitted at no charge.[590]

Whiteway changed hands again in 1936, with Shelbina sports promoter L.B. Thompson taking over with help from Wendell Stultz. They organized a junior league for ages eight to seventeen and a Sunday league.[591] Thompson and Stultz organized an industrial league, with teams from Heisinger Motors, Tweedie's, Miller and Weiss, Walz, Krogers and other merchants.[592]

Thompson also built a girls' softball league and supported the African American Mohawks team.[593]

The Westphalia D-X team poses in 1934 in front of the White Way Park grandstand. White Way Park hosted the Missouri State League games between New Bloomfield, Linn, Lohman, Tebbetts, Russellville, Westphalia and Lloyd's Cleaners and the C.O.B.s, both of Jefferson City. *Photo courtesy of Travis Crede.*

In 1936, Whiteway Park hosted the first Missouri statewide semipro baseball tournament. With the help of the Wichita, Kansas–based National Baseball Congress, the rural park received many new improvements prior to the August 1936, eleven-day tournament. The city's first public address system was installed. Not only was play-by-play announced over the speaker system, but player introductions were made before the game and music played between matches. Also, the Columbia radio station KFRU made the first live game broadcast. Lighting was improved, and the press box was moved to the top of the stands, where a telephone was added.

The National Semi-Pro Baseball Congress had held national tournaments for a few years and was looking for participation from Missouri. Only eight teams from the anticipated twenty-plus invitations had signed up by the July 8 deadline. So Columbia, the original host site, canceled for "lack of interest." The congress office sent its public relations man, Harry "HAP" Peebles, to the Capital City to see the event through.[594]

Peebles set up his temporary office at the sports desk of the *Jefferson City News Tribune*'s four-year-old building downtown. He sent out one hundred invitations to semipro ball clubs statewide, yielding ten more teams.[595]

"Not in the last fifteen years has the city been so enthused over baseball prospects as at the present time," the *Jefferson City Post-Tribune* reported. "Central Missouri baseball fans will be treated to the flashiest brand of baseball ever played on the Capital City diamond....The popular American sport was regaining interest in Jefferson City."[596]

Cardinals scout Gordon "Mae" Maguire was at the tournament for several days, telling the local newspaper he may have found some likely young prospects for the majors.[597]

The double-elimination tournament decided which team would represent the state at the National Semi-Pro Baseball Championship. Over eleven days, twenty-nine games were played by teams from Bonnots Mill, Chamois, Hermann, Iberia, Jefferson City, Kansas City, Mokane, Poplar Bluff, Salem, Sedalia, Springfield, Tipton and Windsor.[598]

The 50 Hiwa Drive-In Theatre opened in 1949 on the former site of the Reed brothers' Whiteway Park. Today, this location of many entertaining events is an open field on Heisinger Road near Missouri Boulevard. *Ad from the* Jefferson City Post-Tribune, *May 31, 1949.*

Former Brooklyn Dodger Zach Wheat, who was living in Polo at the time, opened the tournament, tossing the ball to Mayor Means Ray. Wheat played with the Dodgers for seventeen years with a batting average of .324 and later was a manager.[599]

Youngsters under the age of fifteen were admitted with a membership card for the "Knothole gang" and given their own seating section. Beer was not sold at the park, but spectators could bring in their own buckets.[600]

Local teams included the Capital City Utilities, the Jefferson City Tweedie Shoemen and the Jefferson City Bulldogs. The tournament was integrated, including the local Mohawks, the Tipton Tigers and the ultimate winners, the Kansas City Blackhawks. The local Utilities team, as runners-up, also were invited to the championship tournament.[601]

During the tournament, Utilities batter Frank Triplett "was curving around the bases on his homer inside the park; he was picking them up and laying them down so fast that one of his shoes came off as he came around third base," the *Post-Tribune* reported.[602]

The last mention of Whiteway Park in newspaper accounts is in 1937.[603]

The location was converted into the 50 Hiwa Drive-In Theatre, 727 Heisinger Road, which opened in May 1949. The drive-in was designed by Beverly Miller and Associates, Kansas City, and built by Missouri Valley Steel. The 40-foot-by-56-foot image was projected from a 60-foot-high tower over the 350-car theater. Additional space allowed for another 200 walk-up seats. In 1976, a second screen was added, and the name changed to Twin 50 Drive-In, which closed in September 1985.[604]

PART V

LOST HOMES

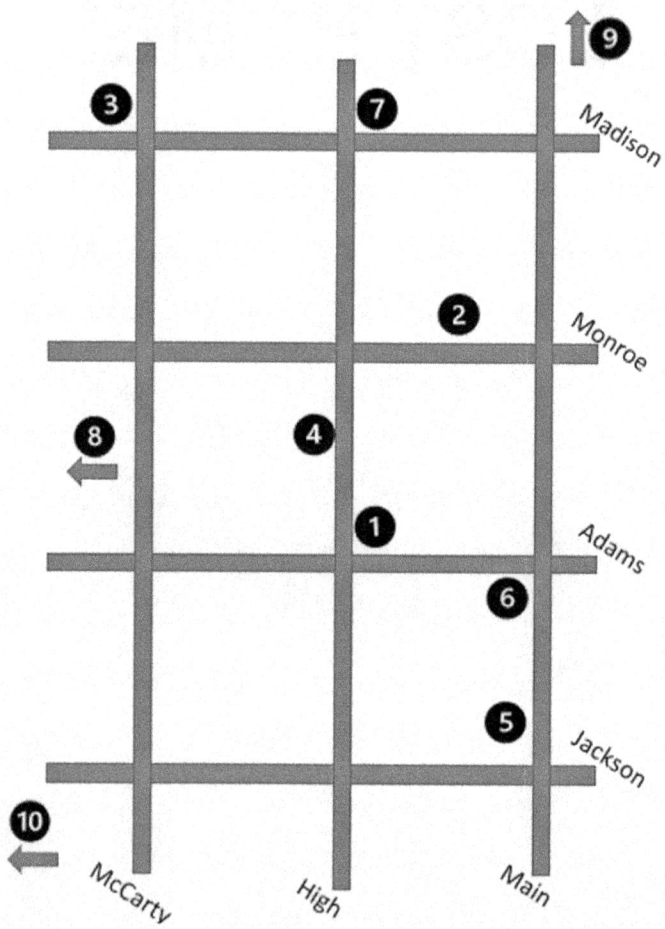

1 Maple Terrace   5 Elston House
2 Summers House   6 Knaup Home
3 Priesmeyer House   7 City Hotel
4 Edwards Home   8 Shoup Home
  Miller Theater   9 Robinson Home
  State Theatre   10 Schoenburg

Map of featured lost homes and businesses in Jefferson City. *Map by Michelle and Stephen Brooks.*

Chapter 20

MAPLE TERRACE

One of the earliest notable homes in uptown Jefferson City was Maple Terrace. Perched on a hill and surrounded by a stone retaining wall topped with a wrought-iron fence, similar to today's Governor's Mansion, the two-story frame home was built in the style of a steamboat with wraparound covered porches on both floors.

Robert William Wells, who designed the Missouri State Seal, also designed this home, which stood until the late 1930s on the corner that now houses the Missouri River Regional Library.

Dr. Robert Young, in his memoirs, recalled Wells as "a brave man, upright judge, good neighbor and sincere friend. On account of his quiet manner and seclusive habits, he was not popular but the few people who did succeed in breaking through his crust of reserve found him a warm-hearted, companionable gentleman."[605]

Wells had practiced law in St. Charles, serving as circuit attorney from 1821 to 1822. His "Great Seal of Missouri" was adopted by the General Assembly on January 11, 1822.

Wells was sent to the House of Representatives 1823–26, joining the first General Assembly to meet in the newly created Capital City. In 1825, he bought ten lots in the city, including the northwest corner of High at Adams, where he built the original log part of what became Maple Terrace.[606]

Wells was elected the state's first attorney general in 1826, serving ten years until the death of Judge James Peck, whom he replaced as the judge of the U.S. District Court for the District of Missouri for the next twenty-one years. When the state was divided into two district courts, he continued another seven years as judge of the U.S. District Court for the Western District until his death in 1864.

Wells heard the 1854 appeal of the Dred Scott case, after the Missouri Supreme Court ruled for the defendant. Wells instructed the jury that to make a decision based on Missouri law, it must also rule in the defendant's favor.

In 1845, Wells also presided over the state's Constitutional Convention.

Wells first bought in 1828 the lot facing High Street, about where the courthouse annex is today. He bought the remaining two lots in the block to the east by 1833. He "held his court in the old County Courthouse," which was just west of his home on the present site.[607]

Involved in the Jefferson City community, Wells became prosecuting attorney for Cole County, was legal adviser to the prison board and served as school superintendent.[608]

During the Civil War, Maple Terrace was known as a center of social activity. By this time, the full vision of the river-packet-inspired home had been reached, including a self-supporting spiral stairway on the front veranda. Two great rooms in the front often were filled with guests, as were the double-decked porches.[609]

Maple Terrace was designed to imitate a riverboat, with two-story wraparound decks and a central stairway. *Photo courtesy of Missouri State Archives, Summers Collection.*

The ample home also quartered Union army officers, in addition to the Wells family and their enslaved people.[610] Wells was a pro-Union Democrat, despite his daughter, Mary, having married Mosby Monroe Parsons, who would become a general in the Confederate States of America.

A Virginia native, Wells married Harriett Amanda (Rector), also a Virginian. She died in 1834, leaving three children. Wells secondly married Eliza (Covington), with whom he had three more children. After the judge's death, Eliza continued to live at Maple Terrace, until she was evicted by creditors.[611]

"The story is told that she defied efforts to move her, although gangs of boys were hired to march about the place banging on old pans and making a general uproar. All these effects failed, but she finally did leave the old building," the *Sunday News and Tribune* reported.[612]

Private schools operated there in the 1870s, including a kindergarten taught by Lizzie Janvier. And Phil White lived there and conducted a private school, while his brother-in-law, Reverend J. Addison Whittaker of the Presbyterian Church, also boarded there.[613]

The home on one and one-half lots sold to Louis Lambert in 1879. Lambert, born in New York, owned a large mill and was a lumber merchant. He was an architectural college graduate and came to St. Louis to build boats on the Mississippi River for the government.

Lambert settled in Castle Rock, Osage County. He represented Osage County one term in the legislature in 1876. Afterward, he remained in Jefferson City six years, engaged in boat construction and at First National Bank before moving to Kansas City.[614]

Alexander Maximillian Beckers, another lumber merchant, bought the home in 1884, moving from a boardinghouse on Madison Street. Born in Westphalia, Beckers opened in 1869 the Chicago Lumber Yard at Main and Jefferson Streets, later called Busch & Beckers and Beckers & Brooks. Future "lumber doctor" Philipp Ott was secretary-treasurer, under Beckers, of the A.M. Beckers Lumber Company.[615]

Beckers was a director of two branch railroad companies and of the Jefferson City Bank. He was a member of the Turner Society and the city shooting club and was elected to the school board in 1878.

Successful merchant Rudolph Dallmeyer bought the home from Beckers in 1886. Until that time, his family had lived above his High Street store, R. Dallmeyer Dry Goods Company.

Dallmeyer was inspired to emigrate from Hanover by his older half brothers, who had returned to Europe on a visit. He arrived in St. Louis at the age of fourteen to work for one of his brothers in the dry goods business. He moved to Jefferson City in 1874, partnering with another brother, William Q., and J.T. Craven in general merchandising.

He married Louise Schmidt, who had worked in the store, on St. Valentine's Day, when the store would be closed, in 1878. Louise's father was Frank Schmidt, who owned the old Madison Hotel. Dallmeyer opened his own store, built for him by Joseph Stampfli, in 1881 at 227 Madison Street.[616]

Dallmeyer moved his growing business in 1886 into another new building constructed for his retail purposes by Hugo Monnig at 206–210 East High Street.[617] The business grew even more when he implemented a cash system. The building was enlarged in 1898 and again in 1908, providing twelve thousand square feet of retail space on two floors. In 1906, its polished oak and modern conveniences made it the "largest and most complete dry goods house in Central Missouri."[618]

Dallmeyer was a councilman, and he was active in home-loan and land organizations. He also had interest in several mining operations.[619] He served three terms as president of the Commercial Club, fighting to keep the capitol in Jefferson City. Dallmeyer was on the club's first board of directors with the charge of building the first Missouri River Bridge, completed in 1896.[620]

Dallmeyer helped entice the Missouri Pacific to add a division here and advocated for the school bond issue for new buildings. He was part of the Commercial Club's effort to help locate three shoe factories outside the Missouri State Penitentiary and to convince Hays Wood Products to remain during World War I.[621]

About 1903, the Dallmeyers moved into a new home built north of Maple Terrace at 214 Adams Street. The pre–Civil War Maple Terrace was then subdivided for rental as residential and association offices.

A fire in the late 1930s claimed the unique home. By 1943, Shell Oil Company had opened a fuel and service station at the busy corner, which was excavated down to street level. The Missouri River Regional Library was later built on this site, when it outgrew the Carnegie Library to the north.

Chapter 21

SUMMERS HOUSE

The last corner to be developed in the block between East Main and East High Streets and Madison and Monroe Streets was at Commercial Way and Monroe. In 1898, the vacant corner was surrounded by brick homes of the well-to-do facing Main Street, the Monroe House and its buildings to the south and the Moore-Bolton Livery to the west.[622]

Land speculator and entrepreneur Oscar Burch had a two-and-a-half-story cement home built at 208 Monroe Street about 1903. The stunning, symmetrical front porch featured rounded gazebos on either corner.

Mary Emma (Blosser) "Mollie" Heskett, who operated a successful millinery at 234 East High Street, bought the home and lot in 1905. Her husband, John, owned the New York Racket Cash Department Store around the corner on East High Street. Before that, they had been renting a house in the 300 block of Monroe Street and taking in boarders.

Both Mollie and John were born in Ohio and then married in Saline County. John graduated from the Missouri State University in 1881, first teaching and then managing his father's large farm.[623] He entered the mercantile business in Malta Bend and then Marshall. He was postmaster in Marshall in 1897, before opening his New York Racket store in Jefferson City.

The store started on Main Street but within two years required a larger space, becoming the largest department store in the county, according to the *1900 Illustrated Sketch Book*.[624] Business was so good, he had to increase his staff from eight to thirty during the holiday season. The rapidly successful store closed by 1904. By 1910, he had opened a new store.

The Summers home once stood where the *Jefferson City News Tribune* upper parking lot is today. *Photo courtesy of Missouri State Archives, Summers Collection.*

The Hesketts continued to take in lodgers in their grand new uptown home. In 1910, lodgers included their future son-in-law, another milliner, a Kentucky minister and Kay Swift, a widow listed as a doctor of medicine.

Mollie died in 1912 from complications from a tooth abscess surgery, but John continued to run the millinery shop at 214 East High Street.

John transferred the home in 1917 to his children, who then sold to Frank Hodges Wymore. Wymore was born in Clay County and his wife, Hilda (Walther), in Cole County. She was the only daughter of noted undertaker and furniture store owner George Walther. The father-in-law and son-in-law became partners in the Walther & Wymore store at 308–312 East High Street.

The young Wymore couple lived with the Walthers at 128 McCarty Street. Then Hilda died, leaving two small children. As a widower, Wymore bought the Monroe Street property in 1917. He remarried in 1918, and they lived in his former father-in-law's home in 1920, the same year he sold the cement mansion to Dr. Joseph Stewart Summers.

Summers was born in Indiana, grew up in Daviess County and brought his medical practice to Jefferson City about 1908.[625] He earned degrees at William Jewell College and the state university and then taught at the latter before becoming a specialist in eye, ear, nose and throat diseases.

Summers first operated his practice out of the Monroe Street home and then moved to the seventh floor of the Central Trust Building by 1925, partnering for a time with his brother-in-law Clarence Pickett and his nephews Dale and Glen Summers. He served inmates at the Missouri State Penitentiary and patients at St. Mary's Hospital.

His wife, Nettie (Pickett), who had completed four years of college, worked as his bookkeeper. Their son, Joe Summers Jr., who was four when the family moved into the Monroe Street mansion, also became a doctor, specializing in radiology.

The Summers family sold to Edward Winter and Robert Goshorn, who built the News Tribune Building at 210 Monroe Street.

Chapter 22

PRIESMEYER HOME

An active and generous man, Henry F. Priesmeyer made Jefferson City his home when he was twenty-one. After studying law in Chicago, Illinois, he followed his uncle, August Priesmeyer, who had partnered with F. Woesten to form A. Priesmeyer & Co.[626]

Priesmeyer was among the entrepreneurs who benefited from the Auburn system of correction, using inmate labor for industries.[627]

The Priesmeyer Boot and Shoe Factory inside the Missouri State Penitentiary is a contributing resource to the historic district listed on the National Register of Historic Places. Built about 1889, the former factory stands west of Housing Unit 2. Once a three-story brick structure, it was rebuilt as a one-story after fire damage from the 1954 riot.[628]

The Missouri State Penitentiary was the center of shoe manufacturing, being the largest producer west of the Alleghenies, Ford's history said.[629] The Priesmeyer operation grew from 35 employees in 1874 to more than 250 in 1900, including 18 national traveling salesmen.[630]

August Priesmeyer was born in Westphalia and immigrated at age seventeen, first to Cincinnati, Ohio, where he learned the shoemaking trade. He then worked at a shoe store in St. Louis until 1859, when he opened his own store. In 1867, he sold his shoe store stock and entered the hide and tobacco business, which failed within two years and sent him back to the shoe business another five years in St. Louis.[631]

Two years after establishing his factory in the prison, August Priesmeyer bought out Woesten in 1874 and continued the operation until 1899.[632]

The Priesmeyer house stands as a reminder of the success and excess of the shoe-manufacturing empire once centered in Jefferson City. *Photo from the 1900* Johnston's Illustrated Sketch Book.

During that time, young Henry Priesmeyer advanced to over-the-road salesman in 1877, took over the office management in 1884 and became finance and sales manager in 1892.[633]

August Priesmeyer retired from active duty with the company about 1891.[634] And in 1899, the business reorganized as the A. Priesmeyer Shoe Company with Henry as secretary-treasurer and business manager. Scottish immigrant John Tweedie Sr., who had been with the company since it began, was made vice president and superintendent.[635]

Henry Priesmeyer died in 1903 and August Priesmeyer in 1905, leaving the business in the hands of Tweedie, who eventually moved it outside the prison and renamed it the Tweedie Footwear Company.[636]

Prominent in civic affairs, Henry Priesmeyer served 1894–95 as president of the Commercial Club, of which he was a charter member.[637] He was the first vice president in 1894 of the Jefferson City Bridge and Transit Company and president of the school board.[638]

Henry Priesmeyer was among the businessmen who developed Cottage Place Park, which hosted community fairs, traveling shows and ball games at the turn of the twentieth century.[639] "He has been active and generous in developing the State Horse Show Association, is fond of baseball, and all the manly sports."[640]

In 1883, Henry Priesmeyer married Julia (Meyer) of St. Charles. By 1891, they were living in a one-and-one-half-story frame house at 402 Madison

Street. By 1900, it had been replaced with a two-and-a-half-story brick house with three chimneys and arched windows, designed by Charles Opel and given the new address of 132 McCarty Street.[641]

After Henry Priesmeyer's death in 1903, the family continued in the home through 1915.[642] Attorneys, doctors and insurance agents occupied the corner home in the 1920s. Then former Cole County circuit clerk Charles Petit replaced the home with one designed by local architect LeRoy Parrish.[643]

Chapter 23

EDWARDS HOME/MILLER THEATER

T he Joseph R. Edwards home at 316 East High Street was a Victorian Gothic–style, two-story brick and stone home, with an arched entry, a two-story turret prominently displayed in the front and a cone-shaped roof.

Edwards' wife, Mary B. (Jefferson), in 1872 bought part of the two-lot estate from her uncle Henry Clay Ewing, who administered the estate of her father, Robert Randolph Jefferson. Her husband bought the remainder of the property the next year from Ewing.

Robert Jefferson and his brother, Meriwether Lewis Jefferson, claimed to be nephews of President Thomas Jefferson. Mary Jefferson's mother was Missouri Jane (Ewing), who was only an infant when her parents came to Jefferson City when it was first platted in 1823.

The son of circuit court judge E.L. Edwards and Ann Ivy (Dixon), Edwards studied at Missouri State University, Columbia, then read law with his father, being admitted to the bar in 1869.[644] Edwards was city assistant attorney before serving 1872–73 as city attorney. He then served 1873–79 as Cole County prosecuting attorney. He was elected city alderman in 1875, mayor in 1883 and Cole County representative in 1892.

Edwards established the *Cole County Democrat* weekly newspaper in 1884, first published in the High Street home built about that same time. Just before 1900, Edwards built the distinctive Democrat Building at the southeast corner of High and Monroe Streets.

The Edwards House stood at 316 East High Street. *Photo from the 1900* Johnston's Illustrated Sketch Book.

As county prosecutor, Edwards assisted Attorney General John Hockaday and Adjutant General George Caleb Bingham in the *State v. General Crafton* case, which saved the federal and state governments hundreds of thousands of dollars.[645] He also was the lead attorney in the case of *State v. Edward Noland*, former state treasurer.

Edwards also was plaintiff and attorney in the injunction suit against the Secretary of State Alexander Lesuer "to restrain him from submitting the amendment for Capital removal."[646]

In the community, Edwards was the original attorney for the Merchant's Bank, as well as a stockholder and director. He was an original incorporator and attorney for the Jefferson City Water Works company. And he was a longtime commander and charter member of the Knights of the Maccabees.

The couple continued the Jefferson name legacy with their son William Jefferson, born 1872, who joined his father's law firm and took over as editor of his father's newspaper in 1900. After Robert's death in 1902, William and his family moved into the family home at 316 East High Street with his mother.[647]

The spacious home was divided and rented by 1908, one side being the residence of Secretary of State John Ephraim Swanger from Buchanan County. After William died at age forty, Mary Jefferson Edwards sold 316 East High Street in 1919 to William "Billy" H. Mueller, a clothing merchant and then restaurant owner who turned to theater management.

MILLER THEATER

By 1922, Mueller had demolished the distinctive home and built the Miller Theater in its place.[648] The new theater could seat more than 1,200 and was a popular place for vaudeville and silent pictures, featuring the theater's own concert orchestra, directed by Cholly Storm.[649]

At the same time, Mueller continued operating the Jefferson Theater at 101 East High Street, which opened as a nickelodeon about 1908, closed by 1935 and was destroyed by fire in 1950.[650]

In 1924, Mueller instituted a new mail-order ticket program to manage the high demand for only two days' showings of Cecil B. DeMille's *The Ten Commandments*.[651]

The Miller Theater was the first to offer "talkies" in Jefferson City in April 1929, showing *Kid Gloves* and a vaudeville short. But recognizing its patrons' interest, the Miller Theater continued hosting vaudeville, Broadway and other live performances every Sunday.[652]

Mueller sold in 1935 to the Dubinsky Brothers, who soon closed the Miller Theater, after opening the Capitol Theater at 111 West High Street, formerly the Krafft Motor Company and Ernest Decker Garage.[653]

The Miller Theater replaced the Edwards House and later was renamed the State Theater. *Photo courtesy of Missouri State Archives, Summers Collection.*

The theater at 316 East High Street reopened by 1941 as the State Theater, under the Durwood theater chain.[654] A novel idea at the time, the State Theater in 1956 began providing child-focused entertainment on Saturday mornings.[655]

By 1960, Jefferson City had four theaters: the State Theater and Capitol Theater on West High Street, as well as the Bridge and 50 Hiwa drive-in theaters.[656]

The historic theater was purchased and then demolished by the Jefferson City Housing Authority in 1969.[657]

Chapter 24

ELSTON HOME

T he Village of Elston was named for the grandparents of George L. Elston, the secretary and director of the L.S. Parker Shoe Company at the turn of the twentieth century.

Andrew M. and Sara Jane (Anthony) Elston arrived in western Cole County about 1828.[658] Their son Dr. Addison Elston, who was George L. Elston's father, married Jane Columbia (Smith).[659] Addison taught school by age sixteen and was deputy for the Cole County and Circuit Courts by seventeen. He studied law with M.M. Parsons until age twenty, when he attended St. Louis Medical College.[660]

After graduation in 1864, Addison Elston served at Jefferson Barracks in St. Louis as a U.S. Army surgeon and later as a commissioned surgeon of the Thirty-First Missouri Volunteer Infantry in Atlanta, Georgia, being part of General William Sherman's March to the Sea.[661]

In 1866, Addison Elston opened his medical practice in Elston and, after additional medical instruction, moved in 1871 to Jefferson City, "where he built a large and lucrative practice."[662]

Not long afterward, Elston recommended to the city council that they have the pond on Main Street drained, and they did so.[663] He also was an original officer of the Medical Society of Central Missouri and served as county coroner.[664]

In 1877, he purchased the former home of E.L. King at the corner of Main and Jackson Streets, described as a "very desirable property, well-suited to the new owner."[665] It had been the home of Andrew Jackson Shockley, a High Street hardware merchant, before that.

The Elston Home once stood at 426 Capitol Avenue. *Photo from the 1900 Johnston's Illustrated Sketch Book.*

Born in Indiana, Shockley was a cooper for Joseph McClurg before his governorship from 1869 to 1871. While in Camden County, he married Rebecca (Tipton) and then returned to Indiana as a farmer. By 1869, he had opened a livery and implement business near Carrollton.[666]

Shockley moved his hardware business in 1875 to Jefferson City, where he also served as the Senate doorkeeper from 1881 to 1887. During that time, he lost his first wife and then married Laura (Ruthven), daughter of J.B. Ruthven, master mason at the Missouri State Penitentiary.[667]

George L. Elston was born in his family's namesake village and spent a lot of time on his grandfather's farm before attending Missouri State University, Columbia. In 1891, he joined L.S. Parker as foreman of the sole leather department for the Jefferson Shoe Company.[668]

The younger Elston jumped to the Star Clothing Manufacturing Company as an officer in 1893, then returned to the L.S. Parker Shoe Company in 1896 as bookkeeper. He was promoted to stockholder and director, as well as secretary, of the latter corporation in 1899. At the same time, he was an officer for the National Association of Accountants. He was described as "a well-balanced young man, of character and integrity."[669]

George and his wife Mary (Brown) lived with his father, Dr. Addison Elston, at 426 West Main Street from 1902 until the latter's death in 1904. Dr. Addison Elston kept poor patient records and left nearly $40,000 of unpaid services on his books at his death, forcing his son to sell the home.[670]

Chapter 25

KNAUP HOME/CITY HOTEL

O ne of the first homes in Jefferson City to have indoor plumbing
was the Italian-style Fred Knaup home at 400 West Main Street.
As owner of the City Hotel, on the northwest corner of Madison
and High Streets, Knaup was one of the wealthiest and most prominent
members of the community.

When Knaup's brother-in-law, Fred Binder, built the modern home on
a prominence visible from roads and rivers outside the city, it was one of
the notable events of the year 1878.[671] The *State Journal* called it "by far
the costliest and best-appointed house in the city…[and] as a specimen of
this line of art, it is a long way ahead of anything in the state, outside of
St. Louis."[672]

The brick home was built on a stone base, trimmed with stone quoins
and galvanized iron trim, with a tin roof and ornate bracketed cornice.
The front and back doors were met with elegant verandahs connected by a
spacious interior hall.[673]

The main floor featured two large parlors separated by sliding doors and a
drawing room and dining room opposite them, as well as a kitchen, laundry,
pantry and administrative offices in the back. The second floor had four
rooms, a bathroom and two rooms for servants.[674]

The attic featured a tank filled hydraulically with water from the cistern,
which then was led into each of the rooms.[675] The bathroom held what is
believed to be the city's first indoor bathtub.[676]

RES. OF F. KNAUP, MAIN STREET.

One of the most celebrated homes in the city was Fred Knaup's, which was one of the first to feature indoor plumbing. *Photo from the 1891* Suden's Sketchbook.

Fifty years after it was built, the Knaup home was remodeled to house KWOS radio station, the first privately owned station in the city, opened by Robert C. Goshorn, owner of the *Jefferson City News Tribune*.[677] Only three years later, in 1940, the home was lost to fire.[678]

Johann Fredrick "Fred" Knaup immigrated to Jefferson City in 1853 at age twenty-two, building carriages and keeping a saloon.[679]

Knaup and his wife, Margaret (Blochberger), devout members of Central Evangelical Church, bought the City Hotel in 1867.[680] With the help of their eldest daughter, Mary, it became a "luxurious and commodious" hotel.[681]

The *People's Tribune* praised Knaup as a "man of great energy and industry...one of the most enterprising, public-spirited men in the city."[682]

After nearly thirty years, Knaup sold the City Hotel, then served as president of Standard Shoe Company, operating inside the Missouri State Penitentiary.[683] The Knaups moved about the turn of the twentieth century from Main Street to 109 Jackson, which Knaup built. (He also built 700 West Main Street.)[684] J.S. Sullivan bought the 400 West Main Street home from Knaup and later sold it to Dr. C.P. Hough.

Knaup served on the city council and twenty-five years on the school board, as well as on the committee to establish a public library.[685] He also was the "unofficial welcomer" for the hundreds of postwar German immigrants, including his brother-in-law, Fred Binder.[686]

CITY HOTEL

As early as 1837, a hotel operated at the northwest corner of Madison and High Streets. By 1845, it was the Marshal House and by 1848 it was the Paulsel House. Michael Newman took over by 1850 and was joined by his son, Harden, by 1860.

Fred Knaup bought part interest in the hotel in 1867, partnering with J.B. Kaiser. During the 1870s, businesses operating inside the City Hotel included Solomon Leopold's clothing, A.H. Wells watches and jewelry, J.I. Levy goods, William Heidt barber, William Rose tobacco, Abe Heim clothing and the *State Journal*.[687]

The City Hotel once stood at the northwest corner of Madison and High Streets, where the Central Trust Building is today. *Photo courtesy of Cole County Historical Society.*

George Wagner sold his brewery and the Wagner Hotel, two doors west on High Street, to Knaup in exchange for the City Hotel in 1874.[688] By 1878, Knaup was the sole owner of the City Hotel again, after J.B. Kaiser took charge of the Madison Hotel on the north end of the same block. At the same time, he "spared neither labor, pain nor expense to suitably arrange the building and most gorgeously furnish it," the *State Journal* reported.[689]

The hotel entrance faced High Street, and Knaup expanded the original building by buying an adjacent building north on Madison, adding eight rooms. Each room featured a suite of walnut furniture topped with marble, built by locals Stampfli & Karges.[690]

Knaup's daughter, Mary, became the landlady, and the kitchen was operated by well-known and respected African American caterer Howard Barnes.[691]

By 1890, George Pope was the hotel's owner. Then Knaup, again owner and in declining health, sold to Ben Vieth and Christ J. Miller, previously liquor dealers, in 1894.[692]

The City Hotel was demolished in 1914 to make way for the Frank Miller–designed Central Trust Building.[693]

Chapter 26

A.C. SHOUP HOME

An odd-looking polygonal home once sat on top of the hill where today's Jefferson City Public School administration building is. The miasma theory popular at the time advocated living high on a hill to promote good health, according to local historian Walter Schroeder. As proponents believed disease was caused by "bad air," a hilltop breeze was optimal.[694]

Alfred C. Shoup and his wife, Emma (Murrain), lived at 327 Dunklin Street, where she was known for her "culture and personal beauty," the *Illustrated Sketch Book* said.[695]

Shoup grew up in Jefferson City, though he was born on an Ohio farm, assisting his father, Henry, who was a wool manufacturer and later an officer at the Missouri State Penitentiary.[696] As a teenager, Shoup apprenticed under local confectioners.[697]

At age seventeen, he apprenticed at the *People's Tribune*, advancing to foreman within two years.[698] He continued for fourteen years with the newspaper's job department, until Henry W. Ewing bought the controlling interest of the Tribune Printing Company and promoted Shoup to business manager of the entire plant, where he remained from 1884 to 1898.[699]

Shoup left the company following Ewing's death, and in 1899, with several others from his previous employer, Shoup organized the Press Printing company, of which he was president and business manager until his death in 1904.

Left: Former mayor Alfred C. Shoup enjoyed fresh air in his home built atop the hill where the Jefferson City Public Schools administration building is today. *Photo from the 1891 Suden's Sketchbook.*

Right: Newspaperman Alfred C. Shoup served two terms as mayor and two as second ward alderman. *Photo from the 1900 Johnston's Illustrated Sketch Book.*

In the community, Shoup served as mayor for two terms and as second ward alderman twice at the turn of the twentieth century.

His obituary said he "was a good man and he enjoyed the friendship of his people."[700]

Chapter 27

G.F. ROBINSON HOME

I rish immigrant George Francis Robinson lived in a spacious home on the western reaches of the city. The L-shaped, double-porched home likely stood between where St. Joseph Bluff Nursing Home and the St. Peter Cemetery are today.[701]

When Robinson died in 1927, the address was listed as 1228 West Main Street. However, street numbering has changed over time in the Capital City.[702]

Robinson arrived in the United States in 1863, working as a hotel clerk in 1870 and a contractor in 1873.[703] He married Perpetia Felicitias (Weiser) in 1871 at St. Peter Church, and then the couple lived with her family through 1880, while he worked as a laborer.[704]

In 1891, he was a clerk in the Jefferson City post office and became postmaster in March 1898, serving five years.[705] The first federal building had been completed in 1889, and city delivery service began in 1890. During Robinson's term, in May 1902, rural delivery was added.[706]

Robinson owned rental property, including an eight-room house at 402 West McCarty Street and a six-room house at 410 West McCarty Street.[707] He also owned property immediately east of the 1889 post office, which was purchased in 1922 by the New Central Hotel Company on the east side of Robinson's property. The land allowed the oldest remaining hotel in the city to build an expansion.[708]

The Robinson family, including children Josephina (b. 1873), Antonnetty (b. 1875), Vielemina (b. 1878) and Frederick (b. 1885), moved into the Charles

The G.F. Robinson House was built on the West Main Street bluff between St. Joseph Nursing Home and St. Peter's Cemetery #3. *Photo from the 1900* Johnston's Illustrated Sketch Book.

Opel–designed West Main Street home before 1900.[709] The home remained in the family, at least through 1940, when Perpetia died and her remains lay in state there before her burial next door at St. Peter's Cemetery.[710]

Local architect Opel built several unique and charming homes in the city, many of which are now gone like the Robinson home. One still standing is the Governor Lon V. Stephens home, more commonly known as Ivy Terrace.[711]

Other architectural works by Opel include homes for attorney Joseph R. Edwards, Captain W.H. Bradbury, shoe baron John Tweedie Sr., grocer M.R. Sinks and manufacturer H.F. Priesmeyer. Opel also built former buildings at Lincoln Institute and for First and Second Baptist Churches, plus several of the finest buildings in Russellville and the Evangelical Church in California, Missouri.[712]

Chapter 28

SCHOENBURG

Perhaps the centerpiece of the Woodcrest subdivision in its glory years, even before it was added to the city limits, was the home of Henry Watkins Ewing, which sat at the center of where StoneBridge Senior Living is today at 1024 Adams Street.

The castellated Gothic-style home was built about 1867 by his uncle, H. Clay Ewing. Henry and Mattie (Chappell) Ewing bought the sixteen-room home, which they called "Schoenburg," about 1883.[713] It was the "envy of town," the *St. Louis Post-Dispatch* said.[714]

Born in Ray County, Henry was valedictorian of Missouri State University–Columbia, class of 1872. His father, Judge E.B. Ewing, who was twice a supreme court judge, and also secretary of state and attorney general, died just a few months after Henry Ewing was admitted to practice law.[715] To help support his widowed and orphaned family, young Henry Ewing was elected clerk of the Missouri Supreme Court, which had only recently been consolidated in Jefferson City, in 1873.[716]

"The court reasoned that they could in no better way attest their friendship for their late associate than to give his son the vacant clerkship, especially since that son was sober, upright, remarkably studious and of considerable attainment in the law," the *St. Louis Post-Dispatch* said.[717]

Henry Ewing had prior government experience as engrossing clerk of the senate and soon made his own mark, known for his handsome dress and unusual shrewdness for his age.[718] He was credited with installing typewriters in the supreme court clerk's office and, at his own expense, published pocket dockets for lawyers.[719]

RES. OF H. W. EWING.

Schoenburg was the first and largest construction on a rise looking north over the city, known today as part of the Woodcrest addition. *Photo from the 1891* Suden's Sketchbook.

"His long and prominent association with capital society has given him polished manners and he is always at ease. His only peculiarity is an assumption of absent-mindedness that sometimes attacks him in the midst of a conversation," the *Post-Dispatch* said.[720]

While serving at the supreme court, Ewing concurrently was part owner at the *Weekly Tribune*, over which he gained a controlling interest in 1883.[721] During his time with the *Weekly Tribune*, it was the official state newspaper, and from 1896 to 1897, Ewing served as president of the Missouri Press Association.[722]

During his time at the state university, Henry Ewing teamed up with his roommate, Eugene Field, and classmate James Cooney to publish the first student newspaper, forerunner to what is today's *Columbia Missourian*.[723] The monthly *University Missourian*'s first eight-page, five-column issue was published on June 23, 1871. Ewing was editor-in-chief, Cooney and J.N. Baskett were assistants and Field was the local and news editor.[724]

The *St. Louis Post-Dispatch* said of Ewing in 1895, he "has accomplished more for himself and his family than any other Missourian under similar circumstances...[being a] clever writer and good business man."[725]

In 1880, he and his wife, Mattie, celebrated the birth of a daughter, who was born the same day and hour as Spanish King Alfonso's daughter. Ewing sent a letter congratulating the royal house on an heiress, and in response, King Alfonso sent an engraved silver cup for the young Ewing.[726]

After Henry Ewing's untimely death, Congressman Dorsey and Florida Lee "Floy" Shackleford bought the Schoenburg in 1901.[727]

Shackleford represented the eighth district from 1899 to 1919.[728] He was elected to fill the unexpired term in the U.S. House of Representatives in August 1899, following the death of Congressman Richard P. "Silver Dick" Bland of Lebanon.[729]

Before his federal service, Shackleford had served seven years as circuit judge and three terms as prosecuting attorney in Cooper County.[730] He was born in Saline County and graduated from William Jewell College–Liberty, before teaching school while studying law.[731]

"While he took an active interest in national affairs, he never forgot the welfare of the district from which he was elected," the *Post-Tribune* said.[732]

Shackleford was chairman of the first-ever congressional committee to study federally funded roads and drafted the Federal Aid Road Act of 1916.[733] He was a strong advocate for road improvements, particularly for rural free delivery of the mail.[734] He opposed the First World War, which lost him the Democratic Party nomination for reelection in 1918.[735]

The unique home, which featured a forty-foot-tall tower on the northeast corner, and extensive land of Schoenburg had been incorporated into the city by 1908, with the address of 314 Franklin Street.[736]

About that time, the Shacklefords sold part of their property to the Schoenburg Land Company, which likely created Oak Street within the Woodcrest Addition, local historian Deborah Goldammer said. Shackleford became a member of the Schoenburg Land Company in 1912, a year before the Woodcrest Addition was filed with the Cole County Recorder.[737]

The next year, 1913, the Shacklefords sold the impressive home and large lot surrounded by the subdivision to Charles and Lillian (Reid) Tweedie. Tweedie was president of Tweedie Footwear at the time. He had entered the shoe business with his father, John Tweedie, after eighth grade at the old Central School on Monroe Street.[738]

"Few men have given as unstintingly of their time and means to improve not only the living conditions of their employees but of the community as a whole. His was a thoroughly useful and worthwhile life," Mayor Jesse Owens said at Tweedie's death.[739]

Tweedie brought an enthusiasm to every undertaking and was remembered for his loyalty, kindness, cheerfulness and "unassuming way of doing things," the Reverend J.A. Vogelweid said.[740]

Charles Tweedie lived in the notable home until his death in 1945, and Lillian lived there a total of fifty-two years, until her death in 1965. Four years later, the home was demolished.[741] A nursing home has operated in its place for more than fifty years.

NOTES

Chapter 1

1. *State Journal* (Jefferson City, MO), July 7, 1876.
2. James E. Ford, *A History of Jefferson City: Missouri's State Capital and of Cole County, Illustrated* (Jefferson City, MO: New Day Press, 1938), 208.
3. W.G. Lyford, *The Western Address Directory* (Baltimore: Jos. Robinson, 1837).
4. Herbert McDougal, St. Joseph newspaper correspondent; Ford, *History of Jefferson City*, 220.
5. *Daily Capital News* (Jefferson City, MO), April 12, 1931.
6. Ford, *History of Jefferson City*, 79.
7. *History of Cole, Moniteau, Morgan, Benton, Miller, Maries and Osage Counties, Missouri* (Chicago: Goodspeed Publishing, 1889).
8. Craig Sturdevant and Gary Kremer, *Jefferson City Historic District Capitol West Mill Bottom* (Jefferson City Housing Authority, 1982), 17.
9. Ibid.
10. Ibid., 20.
11. "History of Jefferson City" folder, Missouri State Archives vertical files, 1973.
12. Sturdevant and Kremer, *Capitol West*, 21.
13. *People's Tribune* (Jefferson City, MO), October 19, 1870.
14. Myrene Houchin Hobbs, *The Jefferson City Story* (Cole County Historical Society, 1956).
15. Sturdevant and Kremer, *Capitol West*.

Chapter 2

16. *History of Cole.*
17. Permanent Seat of Government records, Missouri State Archives.
18. *History of Cole.*
19. *People's Tribune* (Jefferson City, MO), November 1, 1871; Provost Marshal's papers, October 7, 1864, Missouri State Archives.
20. R.E. Young, *Pioneers of High, Water and Main: Reflections of Jefferson City* (Jefferson City: Twelfth State, 1997).
21. Ibid.
22. Ibid.
23. *People's Tribune* (Jefferson City, MO), September 4, 1872.
24. Ibid.
25. Walter Schroeder, *Breweries and Saloons in Jefferson City, Missouri* (Old Munichburg Association, 2009).
26. *Jefferson Inquirer* (Jefferson City, MO), January 2, 1845.
27. Schroeder, *Breweries and Saloons.*
28. Walter Schroeder, notes to the author, September 10, 2021.
29. Ibid.
30. *People's Tribune* (Jefferson City, MO), October 4, 1865.
31. Ibid.
32. *State Republican* (Jefferson City, MO), September 3, 1891.
33. *People's Tribune* (Jefferson City, MO), December 29, 1869.
34. *State Journal* (Jefferson City, MO), September 19, 1873, and January 4, 1878.
35. *State Journal* (Jefferson City, MO), September 19, 1873.
36. Old Breweries, www.oldbreweries.com.
37. "Our Roots Run Deep in Jefferson City," Jefferson City Coca-Cola Bottling Company, https://jccoke.com/our-company/.
38. *State Journal* (Jefferson City, MO), July 14, 1876.
39. *State Republican* (Jefferson City, MO), September 3, 1891.
40. "Our Roots Run Deep."
41. RootsWeb, https://rootsweb.com.
42. *State Republican* (Jefferson City, MO), December 25, 1890.
43. *State Republican* (Jefferson City, MO), May 14, 1891.
44. Schroeder, *Breweries and Saloons.*
45. *State Republican* (Jefferson City, MO), March 10, 1892.
46. *State Republican* (Jefferson City, MO), March 3, 1892.
47. Schroeder, *Breweries and Saloons.*

48. Ibid.
49. Ibid.
50. Ibid.
51. Jacob Schmidt death certificate, Missouri Bureau of Vital Records, Missouri State Archives.
52. *Daily Capital News* (Jefferson City, MO), April 2, 1933.
53. Ibid.
54. Schroeder, *Breweries and Saloons*.
55. Don Whitener, interview with the author, June 29, 2021.
56. *Jefferson City (MO) Post-Tribune*, April 6, 1933.
57. Whitener intervew.
58. *Daily Capital News* (Jefferson City, MO), May 8, 1945; "Ben Fechtel," Cole County, MO, U.S. Census, 1940.
59. Whitener interview.

Chapter 3

60. Guy S. Sone, *G.H. Dulle, His Home and Family* (Jefferson City, 1961).
61. Ibid.
62. Michelle Brooks, *Jefferson City (MO) News Tribune*, June 19, 2016.
63. Sone, *G.H. Dulle*; *People's Tribune*, July 12, 1876.
64. Sone, *G.H. Dulle*.
65. Michelle Brooks, *Jefferson City (MO) News Tribune*, June 19, 2016.
66. Ibid.
67. Ibid.
68. Cole County Genealogy, www.colecountygenealogy.com/civil-war.html.
69. Michelle Brooks, *Jefferson City (MO) News Tribune*, June 19, 2016.
70. *People's Tribune* (Jefferson City, MO), January 10, 1866.
71. *State Journal* (Jefferson City, MO), June 27, 1873.
72. H.H. Altgilbers, Cole County, MO, U.S. Census, 1880.
73. New Orleans, Passenger List, 1813–1963.
74. St. Peter Benevolent Society files, St. Peter Catholic Church Archives.
75. Ibid.; *People's Tribune* (Jefferson City, MO), July 10, 1878.
76. *People's Tribune* (Jefferson City, MO), May 24, 1871.
77. J.W. Johnston, *The Illustrated Sketch Book and Directory of Jefferson City and Cole County* (Jefferson City: Missouri Illustrated Sketch Book Company, 1900).

78. Sone, *G.H. Dulle*.
79. *State Journal* (Jefferson City, MO), June 27, 1873.
80. Sanborn Map Company, Jefferson City, MO, 1892.
81. *Gould's St. Louis Directory*, 1878.
82. *State Journal* (Jefferson City, MO), August 10, 1877.
83. *Gould's St. Louis Directory*, 1878.
84. *Gould's St. Louis Directory*, 1881.
85. Jane Beetem, "Joseph and Elizabeth Wallendorf House," National Register of Historic Places, 2008.
86. Journal of the General Assembly, Missouri State Archives, 1843, 1871.
87. *People's Tribune* (Jefferson City, MO), May 22, 1872.
88. *State Republican* (Jefferson City, MO), October 5, 1893.
89. Ibid.
90. Jane Beetem, "Dr. Joseph P. and Effie Porth House," National Register of Historic Places, 2001.
91. Sone, *G.H. Dulle*.
92. Sturdevant and Kremer, *Capitol West*.
93. Sanborn Map Company, Jefferson City, MO, 1892.
94. Sturdevant and Kremer, *Capitol West*.
95. Ibid.
96. Sanborn Map Company, Jefferson City, MO, 1898
97. Sturdevant and Kremer, *Capitol West*; *Jefferson City Souvenir, Past and Present Progress and Prosperity* (Hugh Stephens Printing, 1912).
98. *Jefferson City Souvenir*.
99. Johnston, *Illustrated Sketch Book and Directory*.
100. *Polk's Jefferson City Directory*, 1929.
101. *New Day Press City Directory*, Jefferson City, MO, 1951.
102. *Hoye's Jefferson City, MO, City Directory*, 1904.
103. *Gould's St. Louis Directory*, 1881
104. Walter Schroeder, letter to the author, December 15, 2019.
105. *State Republican* (Jefferson City, MO), July 4, 1895.

Chapter 4

106. *State Journal* (Jefferson City, MO), June 19, 1874.
107. "New Buildings," *State Journal* (Jefferson City, MO), January 4, 1878.
108. Ibid.
109. Sanborn Map Company, Jefferson City, MO, 1885 and 1892.

110. *Jefferson City (MO) Post-Tribune*, June 6, 1935.
111. *Jefferson City (MO) Post-Tribune*, October 2, 1934.
112. *Jefferson City (MO) Post-Tribune*, February 19, 1940.
113. *Jefferson City (MO) Post-Tribune*, March 8, 1939.
114. *Jefferson City (MO) Post-Tribune*, January 4, 1935.
115. *Jefferson City (MO) Post-Tribune*, January 8, 1935.
116. Sanborn Map Company, Jefferson City, MO, 1916.
117. *Daily Capital News* (Jefferson City, MO), November 25, 1933.
118. Michelle Brooks, "Henry Wallau," Cole County History series, *Jefferson City (MO) News Tribune*, July 10, 2021.
119. *Sedalia (MO) Democrat*, October 16, 1897.
120. William D. Kay, Tennessee death certificate, 1918.
121. *Jefferson City (MO) Post-Tribune*, March 5, 1936.
122. Brooks, "Henry Wallau."
123. Ibid.
124. Ibid.
125. St. Peter Church archives.
126. Ibid.
127. Brooks, "Henry Wallau."
128. Ibid.
129. *Jefferson City Souvenir*.
130. *Jefferson City (MO) Post Tribune*, August 21, 1941.
131. *Jefferson City (MO) Post Tribune*, September 18, 1941.
132. *Jefferson City (MO) Post Tribune*, August 21, 1941.
133. Ibid.
134. Ibid.
135. "Anna Angenendt Norwood," Cole County Historical Society, www.colecohistsoc.org/bios/bio_n.html.
136. *Jefferson City (MO) Post Tribune*, August 21, 1941.
137. "Anna Angenendt Norwood."
138. *Jefferson City (MO) Post Tribune*, July 15, 1930.
139. Ibid.
140. Jackie Haar Trippensee, "Frank H. Rephlo," Ancestry.com.
141. Ibid.
142. Ibid.
143. *Sunday News and Tribune* (Jefferson City, MO), December 30, 1945.
144. *Jefferson City (MO) Post Tribune*, June 17, 1960.
145. *Jefferson City (MO) Post Tribune*, February 23, 1943.
146. *Sunday News and Tribune* (Jefferson City, MO), December 30, 1945.

147. *Sunday News Tribune* (Jefferson City, MO), June 1, 1975.

148. Ibid.

149. Ibid.

Chapter 5

150. Michelle Brooks, *Hidden History of Jefferson City* (Charleston, SC: The History Press, 2021).

151. Ibid.

152. Ibid.

153. *Daily Capital News* (Jefferson City, MO), May 31, 1931.

154. *People's Tribune* (Jefferson City, MO), December 18, 1867.

155. *People's Tribune* (Jefferson City, MO), April 24, 1872.

156. *State Republican* (Jefferson City, MO), March 23, 1894.

157. *People's Tribune* (Jefferson City, MO), June 2, 28, 1871.

158. Wayne Johnson, spreadsheet of early city elected officials, 2021.

159. *Jefferson City (MO) Post-Tribune*, November 25, 1953.

160. Ibid.; *Jefferson City (MO) Post-Tribune*, July 12, 1930.

161. *Jefferson City (MO) Post-Tribune*, July 12, 1930.

162. *Sunday News and Tribune* (Jefferson City, MO), July 6, 1958.

163. *Sunday News and Tribune* (Jefferson City, MO), October 4, 1936.

164. *Jefferson City (MO) Post Tribune*, October 31, 1930.

165. *Daily Capital News* (Jefferson City, MO), April 19, 1931.

166. *Sunday News and Tribune* (Jefferson City, MO), July 6, 1958.

167. *Daily Capital News* (Jefferson City, MO), March 22, 1925.

168. *Daily Capital News* (Jefferson City, MO), February 11, 1931.

169. *Sunday News and Tribune* (Jefferson City, MO), November 4, 1934.

170. *Sunday News and Tribune* (Jefferson City, MO), July 6, 1958.

171. Michelle Brooks, "Landmark Diminished Threat of Relocating Capitol," *Jefferson City (MO) News Tribune*, Landmark series, December 19, 2010.

172. Michelle Brooks, "Cole County History," presented to Learning In Retirement, 2019.

173. Ibid.

174. Ibid.

175. Ibid.

176. Brooks, "Landmark Diminished Threat."

177. Brooks, "Cole County History."

178. Brooks, "Landmark Diminished Threat."
179. Brooks, "Cole County History."
180. *Sunday News and Tribune* (Jefferson City, MO), December 3, 1933.
181. *State Republican* (Jefferson City, MO), June 25, 1891.
182. *Sunday News and Tribune* (Jefferson City, MO), December 3, 1933.
183. Ibid.
184. Ibid.
185. *Sunday News and Tribune* (Jefferson City, MO), September 14, 1947.
186. *Sunday News and Tribune* (Jefferson City, MO), October 6, 1935.
187. *Sunday News and Tribune* (Jefferson City, MO), December 3, 1933.
188. Ibid.
189. *Sunday News and Tribune* (Jefferson City, MO), September 14, 1947.
190. *Sunday News and Tribune* (Jefferson City, MO), October 6, 1935.
191. *St. Joseph (MO) Gazette*, November 24, 1913.
192. Undated clipping, Cole County Historical Society.
193. Ibid.
194. *Jefferson City (MO) Post-Tribune*, March 28, 1934.
195. Undated clipping, Cole County Historical Society.
196. *People's Tribune* (Jefferson City, MO), August 30, 1871.
197. *People's Tribune* (Jefferson City, MO), September 6, 1871.
198. Ibid.
199. *People's Tribune* (Jefferson City, MO), August 30, 1871.
200. *State Journal* (Jefferson City, MO), April 25, 1873.
201. *State Journal* (Jefferson City, MO), October 16, 1874.
202. *People's Tribune* (Jefferson City, MO), Jun 16, 1875.
203. *State Republican* (Jefferson City, MO), June 13, 1895.
204. "MoPac's First 125 Years," Missouri Pacific Historical Society, www.mopac.org.
205. *Jefferson City (MO) Post-Tribune*, September 17, 1929.
206. "MoPac's First 125 Years."

Chapter 6

207. Nancy Arnold Thompson, "Emancipated Woman One of Earliest Landholders," Cole County History series, *Jefferson City (MO) News Tribune*, March 14, 2020.
208. Ibid.
209. Ibid.

210. Ibid.

211. Ibid.; Gary Kremer, "Missouri's Black Historic Sites: A View Over Time," Missouri Department of Natural Resources, 1982.

212. Thompson, "Emancipated Woman."

213. Ibid.

214. Ibid.

215. Ibid.

216. Kremer, "Missouri's Black Historic Sites."

217. Ibid.

218. Ibid.

219. Ibid.

220. Ibid.

221. Ibid.

222. Carolyn Bening, "The Hagen/Hiram Brooks House—A Lost Cultural Heritage," Cole County History series, *Jefferson City (MO) News Tribune*, June 29, 2019.

223. Kremer, "Missouri's Black Historic Sites."

224. Ibid.

225. Ibid.

226. Ibid.

227. Ibid.

228. Johnston, *Illustrated Sketch Book and Directory*, 163.

229. *Daily Capital News* (Jefferson City, MO), September 22, 1928.

230. *Daily Capital News* (Jefferson City, MO), April 2, 1929.

231. Kremer, "Missouri's Black Historic Sites."

Chapter 7

232. Kremer, "Missouri's Black Historic Sites."

233. Michelle Brooks, "Rep. Walthall Moore," *Jefferson City (MO) News Tribune*, 2021.

234. Kenneth Logan, interview with John Viessman and Henry Gensky, Missouri State Museum oral history.

235. Ibid.

236. Victor H. Green, *The Negro Motorist Green Book*, 1941.

237. *Lincoln Clarion* (Jefferson City, MO), April 27, 1945.

238. Victor H. Green, *The Negro Motorist Green Book*, 1947.

239. *Lincoln Clarion* (Jefferson City, MO), April 27, 1945.

240. Ibid.
241. *Lincoln Clarion* (Jefferson City, MO), May 18, 1945.
242. *Lincoln Clarion* (Jefferson City, MO), April 27, 1945.
243. Ibid.
244. Eric Kelley, interview with Janet Maurer, Historic City of Jefferson/ Missouri Department of Transportation, May 11, 2017.
245. *Lincoln Clarion* (Jefferson City, MO), March 20, 1953.
246. "Rufus Petty," WWI records, Fold3.com.
247. "Rufus Petty," Cole County, MO, U.S. Census, 1930.
248. *Lincoln Clarion* (Jefferson City, MO), February 14, 1951.
249. Peggy Williams, interview for Historic City of Jefferson/Missouri Department of Transportation, 2017.
250. Ibid.
251. Perry Douglas, interview for Historic City of Jefferson/Missouri Department of Transportation, 2017.
252. Williams interview.
253. Douglas interview.
254. Glover Brown Jr., interview for Historic City of Jefferson/Missouri Department of Transportation, 2017.
255. Williams interview.
256. Glover Brown Jr. interview.
257. Ibid.
258. Raymond F. Tisby, "Tayes Three Times a Grad, Talented, Colorful, Illustrious," *Lincoln Clarion* (Jefferson City, MO), May 15, 1953.
259. Ibid.
260. Ibid.
261. Member #47312304, "Ulysses S. Grant Tayes," Findagrave.com
262. Peter Hasting Falk, *Who Was Who in American Art* (Madison, CT: Sound View Press, 1999).
263. The Foot African American History Project Committee.
264. Tisby, "Tayes Three Times a Grad."
265. "Grant Tayes Recognized as a Real Artist," *Jefferson City (MO) Post Tribune*, September 2, 1931.
266. Tisby, "Tayes Three Times a Grad."
267. *Leshnick's City Directory of Jefferson City*, 1921.
268. Tisby, "Tayes Three Times a Grad."
269. *Leshnick's City Directory.*
270. Tisby, "Tayes Three Times a Grad."
271. "Grant Tayes Recognized."

272. Tisby, "Tayes Three Times a Grad."

273. Ibid.

274. Ibid.

Chapter 8

275. The Foot African American History Project Committee.

276. *Lincoln Clarion* (Jefferson City, MO), October 21, 1955.

277. Glover Brown Jr. interview.

278. Ibid.

279. Arthur Brown, interview for Historic City of Jefferson/Missouri Department of Transportation, 2017.

280. Ibid.

281. Ibid.

282. Gloria Kelley Brent, interview with Janet Maurer, Historic City of Jefferson/Missouri Department of Transportation, May 8, 2017.

283. Gary Kremer, interview with Vicki Schildmeyer, Historic City of Jefferson/Missouri Department of Transportation, June 6, 2017.

284. Ibid.

285. Ibid.

286. Ibid.

287. *Daily Capital News* (Jefferson City, MO), January 9, 1964.

288. Ibid.

289. *Daily Capital News* (Jefferson City, MO), October 16, 1947.

290. *Lincoln Clarion* (Jefferson City, MO), October 4, 1950.

291. The Foot African American History Project Committee, 2021.

292. Ibid.

293. Ibid.

294. Ibid.

295. Ibid.

296. Ibid.

297. Ibid.

298. Kenneth Logan interview.

299. Ibid.; Joyce Logan Webb, interview with the author, June 3, 2021.

300. Kenneth Logan interview.

301. Ibid.

302. Find a Grave, https://www.findagrave.com.

303. Ibid.

304. Ibid.

305. Ibid.

306. Joyce Logan Webb interview.

307. *Sunday News and Tribune* (Jefferson City, MO), November 21, 1965.

308. Michelle Brooks, "Officer Wallace Lawson, Jefferson City's First Police Officer Killed in Line of Duty," Cole County History series, *Jefferson City News Tribune*, August 1, 2020.

309. Ibid.

310. Ibid.

311. *Jefferson City (MO) Post Tribune*, May 10, 1934.

312. *Jefferson City (MO) Post Tribune*, February 8, 1937.

313. Ibid.

314. *Jefferson City (MO) Post Tribune*, February 18, 1941.

315. *Daily Capital News* (Jefferson City, MO), May 7, 1932.

316. *Sunday News and Tribune* (Jefferson City, MO), September 7, 1958.

Chapter 9

317. William Bailey, "Vets' Cab Serves LU and City," *Lincoln Clarion* (Jefferson City, MO), September 26, 1947.

318. Ibid.

319. *Lincoln Clarion* (Jefferson City, MO), May 17, 1946.

320. Reports of Separation Notices, 1941–1946, Missouri, Missouri State Archives.

321. World War II draft card, Fold3.com, October 16, 1940.

322. The Foot African American History Project Committee.

323. "Hulen Henderson," Cole County, MO, U.S. Census, 1940.

324. *Daily Capital News* (Jefferson City, MO), June 12, 1946.

325. Don Webb, interview with the author, June 11, 2021.

326. *Lincoln Clarion* (Jefferson City, MO), May 4, 1949.

327. "Norman Bolton," World War I draft card, 1918.

328. *Lincoln Clarion* (Jefferson City, MO), May 4, 1949.

329. *Jefferson City (MO) News Tribune*, March 26, 1950.

330. Bob Baysinger, *Sunday News and Tribune* (Jefferson City, MO), June 8, 1969.

331. Ibid.

332. Michelle Brooks, "'Lefty' Robinson, the King of Jefferson City Mohawk Baseball," Cole County History series, *Jefferson City (MO) News Tribune*, November 23, 2019.

333. Baysinger.

334. *Lincoln Clarion* (Jefferson City, MO), October 20, 1944.

335. *Jefferson City Post-Tribune*, February 17, 1950.

336. Brooks, "'Lefty' Robinson."

337. *Sunday News and Tribune*, February 6, 1966.

338. Brooks, "'Lefty' Robinson."

339. Ibid.

Chapter 10

340. Leona Rice interview, Missouri State Museum oral history.

341. Ibid.

342. Douglas interview.

343. Rice interview.

344. Brown interview.

345. Rice interview.

346. Ibid.

347. Douglas interview.

348. World War II Draft Registration for Missouri.

349. *Lincoln Clarion* (Jefferson City, MO), December 14, 1949.

350. *Daily Capital News* (Jefferson City, MO), September 24, 1942.

351. *Lincoln Clarion* (Jefferson City, MO), April 23, 1948.

352. *Lincoln Clarion* (Jefferson City, MO), January 11, 1946.

353. Ibid.

354. Ibid.

355. Ibid.

356. *Lincoln Clarion.* (Jefferson City, MO), March 8, 1950.

357. *Lincoln Clarion* (Jefferson City, MO), May 2, 1951.

358. *Jefferson City (MO) Post Tribune*, July 3, 1929.

359. *Lincoln Clarion* (Jefferson City, MO), October 3, 1947.

360. Ibid.

361. *Lincoln Clarion* (Jefferson City, MO), March 16, 1949.

362. *Lincoln Clarion* (Jefferson City, MO), March 9, 1949.

363. *Lincoln Clarion* (Jefferson City, MO), October 3, 1947.

364. *Daily Capital News* (Jefferson City, MO), June 13, 1934; *Jefferson City Directory*, 1933.

365. *Jefferson City (MO) Post Tribune*, May 27, 1949.

366. Don Webb, interview with the author, June 11, 2021.

367. Arthur Brown interview.
368. Glover Brown Jr. interview.
369. Ibid.
370. Don Webb interview.
371. Ibid.
372. *Jefferson City (MO) Post Tribune*, May 2, 1969.
373. Glover Brown Jr. interview.
374. Ibid.
375. Arthur Brown interview.
376. Glover Brown Jr. interview.

Chapter 12

377. Gail Severance, email to the author.
378. Brooks, *Hidden History of Jefferson City*.
379. *State Journal* (Jefferson City, MO), November 3, 1876.
380. Severance email.
381. Ibid.
382. Ibid.
383. Richard Edwards, *1869 City Directory, St. Louis*, www.digital.wustl.edu.
384. *State Journal* (Jefferson City, MO), January 4, 1878.
385. *Indiana State Sentinel*, February 28, 1883.
386. Johnston, *Illustrated Sketch Book and Directory*. 417.
387. Ibid., 156.
388. *Jefferson City Post-Tribune*, February 10, 1917.
389. Severance email.
390. Ibid.

Chapter 13

391. *State Journal* (Jefferson City, MO), November 16, 1877.
392. *State Journal* (Jefferson City, MO), February 8, 1878.
393. Ibid.
394. *State Journal* (Jefferson City, MO), November 16, 1877.
395. USCT enlistment papers, Fold3.com.
396. *Macon (MO) Times Democrat*, July 29, 1915.
397. *Sedalia (MO) Weekly Conservator*, June 9, 1906.

398. Floyd Shoemaker, "Governor's Ball High Social Event," *Sikeston (MO) Herald*, February 22, 1945.

399. E.M. Watson, *State Republican* (Jefferson City, MO), December 18, 1890.

400. *State Republican* (Jefferson City, MO), December 18, 1890.

401. *Daily Capital News* (Jefferson City, MO), January 26, 1966.

402. Arnold Parks, *Lincoln University: 1920–1970* (Charleston, SC: Arcadia Publishing, 2007).

403. Michelle Brooks, *Jefferson City (MO) News Tribune*, February 5, 2017.

404. *State Republican* (Jefferson City, MO), December 18, 1890; *Osage Valley Banner*, September 30, 1880.

405. Nancy Arnold Thompson, email to the author, April 17, 2021.

406. Walter Schroeder, email to Nancy Arnold Thompson, 2021.

407. Thompson email.

408. Nancy Arnold Thompson, "Proof of Burials," unpublished, 2021.

409. *Jefferson City (MO) Post-Tribune*, July 9, 1931.

410. *Daily Capital News* (Jefferson City, MO), May 8, 1934.

411. *Jefferson City (MO) Post-Tribune*, October 19, 1931.

412. *Daily Capital News* (Jefferson City, MO), October 3, 1933.

413. *Daily Capital News* (Jefferson City, MO), September 15, 1936.

414. Brooks, *Hidden History of Jefferson City*.

415. Cole County, MO, Probate, May 5, 1914.

416. *Yesterday and Today*, newsletter published by the Historic City of Jefferson, November 2017.

417. *Jefferson City (MO) Post-Tribune*, November 27, 1929.

418. Ibid.

419. *Jefferson City (MO) Post-Tribune*, January 4, 1935.

Chapter 14

420. *Central United Church of Christ Jefferson City, Missouri: A Sesquicentennial History, 1858–2008* (Marceline, MO: Walsworth, 2008).

421. Ibid.

422. Ibid.

423. Ibid.

424. Ibid.

425. Walter Schroeder, Landmark nomination, 2008.

426. Johnston, *Illustrated Sketch Book and Directory*.

427. *A Sesquicentennial History*.

428. Ibid.

429. Ibid.

430. Ibid.

431. Ibid.

432. Ibid.

433. George Walz, "To Make Way for Highway," *Jefferson City (MO) News Tribune,* January 3, 1965.

434. Ibid.

435. *A Sesquicentennial History.*

436. Schroeder, Landmark nomination.

437. Ibid.

438. *A Sesquicentennial History.*

439. Ibid.

440. Thompson email.

441. *A Sesquicentennial History.*

442. Ibid.

Chapter 15

443. Louis Menks, *Cemeteries in Cole County, Missouri, as Recorded in the 1930s,* 104.

444. *St. Peter Catholic Church, 1883–1983* (Jefferson City, 1983).

445. History of Resurrection Cemetery, courtesy of Nancy Arnold Thompson.

446. Menks, *Cemeteries in Cole County.*

447. Alan Lepper, interview with Nancy Arnold Thompson, 2021.

448. Ibid.

449. Gilbert J. Garraghan, *The Jesuits of the Middle United States* (Chicago: Loyola University Press, 1983), 447.

450. Ibid.

451. Reverend John Buchanan, letter to Alma Eggen, Loose Creek, February 1, 1980.

452. *History of Resurrection Cemetery.*

453. Menks, *Cemeteries in Cole County.*

454. Ibid.

455. Buchanan letter.

456. Ibid.

457. Thompson email.

458. Dorothy Kemper, St. Peter's Cemetery Records, 1977.

459. Ibid.

Chapter 16

460. *People's Tribune* (Jefferson City, MO), October 10, 1866.

461. *Missouri State Times* (Jefferson City, MO), May 30, 1863.

462. *People's Tribune* (Jefferson City, MO), October 11, 1865.

463. *People's Tribune* (Jefferson City, MO), January 24, 1866.

464. *People's Tribune* (Jefferson City, MO), August 29, 1866.

465. *Weekly People's Tribune* (Jefferson City, MO), September 8, 1869.

466. "John W. Giesecke Recalls Attractions at Old City Fairgrounds," Cole County Historical Society series, *Sunday News and Tribune* (Jefferson City, MO), January 26, 1947.

467. *State Journal* (Jefferson City, MO), June 30, 1875.

468. "Giesecke Recalls Attractions."

469. *State Journal* (Jefferson City, MO), September 17, 1875.

470. *State Republican* (Jefferson City, MO), July 7, 1892.

471. "Giesecke Recalls Attractions."

472. *State Republican* (Jefferson City, MO), September 27, 1894.

473. *State Republican* (Jefferson City, MO), July 28, September 8, 1892.

474. "Giesecke Recalls Attractions."

475. *State Journal* (Jefferson City, MO), June 23, 1876; Pat Kliethermes, interview with the author, August 19, 2021.

476. *State Journal* (Jefferson City, MO), June 23, 1876.

477. Brooks, "Cole County History."

478. *St. Louis (MO) Republican*, October 9, 1876.

479. *Cole County Deeds Book R* (1821–1870), 585.

480. *State Republican* (Jefferson City, MO), October 19, 1893.

481. *State Republican* (Jefferson City, MO), August 30, 1894.

482. "Lack of Funds Lost Jefferson City its Parks of Yesteryear," Cole County Historical Society series, *Sunday News and Tribune* (Jefferson City, MO), December 22, 1946.

483. "Many Jefferson Citians Owned Fast Horses and Made East Main Street a Race Track," Cole County Historical Society series, *Sunday News and Tribune* (Jefferson City, MO), February 2, 1947.

484. Lawrence Lutkewitte, *Jefferson City (MO) Post-Tribune*, April 19, 1931.

485. Michelle Brooks, Landmarks series, *Jefferson City (MO) News Tribune*.

486. Lutkewitte.

487. Ibid.

488. *Jefferson City (MO) Post-Tribune*, December 14, 1933.

489. Ford, *History of Jefferson City*.

490. *Jefferson City (MO) Post-Tribune*, December 14, 1933.

491. Brooks, Landmarks series.

492. Minnie Haughn Boyce, "Her Historical Wardrobe," *Jefferson City (MO) Tribune*, March 9, 1947.

Chapter 17

493. *Daily Capital News* (Jefferson City, MO), April 26, 1931.

494. George Hope Jr., "Horse Shows, Flower Shows and Baseball at Cottage Park," Cole County Historical Society column, *Jefferson City (MO) News and Tribune*, April 13, 1947.

495. Ibid.

496. Ibid.

497. Ibid.

498. Ibid.

499. *Daily Capital News* (Jefferson City, MO), April 26, 1931.

500. Hope, "Horse Shows, Flower Shows and Baseball."

501. *State Republican* (Jefferson City, MO), May 21, 1896.

502. Hope, "Horse Shows, Flower Shows and Baseball."

503. Mark O'Neill, "O'Neill and the St. Louis Browns of 1887."

504. *Jefferson City (MO) Daily Tribune*, April 17, 1909.

505. Johnston, *Illustrated Sketch Book and Directory*.

506. Ibid.

507. Ibid.

508. *St. Louis (MO) Post-Dispatch*, July 7, 1895.

509. Johnston, *Illustrated Sketch Book and Directory*.

510. Ibid.

511. Johnston, *Illustrated Sketch Book and Directory*.

512. Ibid.

513. Ibid.

514. *St. Louis (MO) Post-Dispatch*, May 14, 1900.

515. *Yesterday and Today*, Historic City of Jefferson, May 2018.

516. Hope, "Horse Shows, Flower Shows and Baseball."

517. Ibid.; *Yesterday and Today*.

518. Ibid.

Chapter 18

519. *Jefferson City (MO) Daily News,* January 28, 1909.
520. *Jefferson City (MO) Daily News,* April 17, 1909.
521. Michelle Brooks, "Henry Ruwart Sr.," Ancestry.com.
522. Brooks, *Hidden History of Jefferson City.*
523. *Jefferson City (MO) Post-Tribune,* December 5, 1961.
524. *Daily Capital News* (Jefferson City, MO), May 21, 1920.
525. *St. Louis (MO) Globe-Democrat,* July 29, 1923.
526. *Iron County (Ironton, MO) Register,* January 8, 1914.
527. *Brazel (IN) Daily Times,* January 16, 1915.
528. Brooks, "Henry Ruwart Sr."
529. *Daily Capital News* (Jefferson City, MO), May 21, 1920.
530. "Leslie and Sons Purchased the Ruwart Motor Company Yesterday," *Daily Capital News* (Jefferson City, MO), January 21, 1923.
531. "Conscientious Service Motto of Blackwell," *Sunday News and Tribune* (Jefferson City, MO), June 9, 1935.
532. House and Senate Journals, 51st General Assembly, 1921 Senate Journal, First Regular Session and Extra Session, Missouri Digital Heritage, 1921.
533. Ibid.
534. Ibid.
535. Ibid.
536. Ibid.
537. Ibid.
538. Ibid.
539. Ibid.
540. Ibid.
541. *Kansas City (MO) Journal,* January 23, 1899.
542. *St. Louis (MO) Post-Dispatch,* January 22, 1922.
543. *Daily Capital News* (Jefferson City, MO), April 26, 1931.
544. *Daily Capital News* (Jefferson City, MO), June 21, 1921.
545. St. Mary's College *Dial* Yearbook, 1923, https://www.e-yearbook.com.
546. *Daily Capital News* (Jefferson City, MO), April 26, 1931.
547. *Jefferson City (MO) Post-Tribune,* April 12, 1937; *Daily Capital News* (Jefferson City, MO), May 30, 1920; Lawrence Lutkewitte, "Jefferson City's Third Ball Park Is the Largest," *Jefferson City (MO) Post-Tribune,* April 26, 1931.
548. "Sedalia in a League?" *Sedalia (MO) Democrat,* January 9, 1910.

549. *Chillicothe (MO) Constitution-Tribune*, April 8, 1911.
550. *Sunday News and Tribune* (Jefferson City, MO), June 8, 1969.
551. Ibid.
552. Ibid.
553. *Daily Capital News* (Jefferson City, MO), June 14, 1921.
554. *Jefferson City (MO) Post-Tribune*, June 10, 1929; *Springfield (MO) News-Leader*, August 15, 1974; *Jefferson City (MO) Post-Tribune*, April 12, 1937.

Chapter 19

555. *Daily Capital News* (Jefferson City, MO), April 26, 1931.
556. *Jefferson City (MO) Post-Tribune*, September 18, 1930.
557. Brooks, "Cole County History."
558. Michelle Brooks, "Open Field Once Held Community Athletic Events," Cole County History series, *Jefferson City (MO) News Tribune.*
559. Ibid.
560. *Jefferson City (MO) Post-Tribune*, August 29, 1930.
561. Ibid.
562. Brooks, "Open Field."
563. *Jefferson City (MO) Post-Tribune*, May 15, 1931.
564. Ibid.
565. *Jefferson City (MO) Post-Tribune*, July 1, 1931.
566. *Jefferson City (MO) Post-Tribune*, July 2, 1931.
567. Yendis Pencilette, *Jefferson City (MO) Post-Tribune*, September 25, 1930.
568. *Jefferson City (MO) Post-Tribune*, July 14, 1931.
569. *Daily Capital News* (Jefferson City, MO), September 25, 1932.
570. *Jefferson City (MO) Post-Tribune*, September 29, 1930.
571. *Jefferson City (MO) Post-Tribune*, October 4, 1930.
572. *Jefferson City (MO) Post-Tribune*, September 17, 1931.
573. Brooks, "Open Field."
574. *Jefferson City (MO) Post-Tribune*, July 15, 1931.
575. *Jefferson City (MO) Post-Tribune*, July 17, 1931.
576. *Jefferson City (MO) Post-Tribune*, July 18, 1931.
577. Lawrence Lutkewitte, *Daily Capital News* (Jefferson City, MO), April 19, 1931.
578. *Jefferson City (MO) Post-Tribune*, May 5, 1931.
579. *Jefferson City (MO) Post-Tribune*, March 12, 1931.
580. *Jefferson City (MO) Post-Tribune*, May 11, 1931.

581. *Daily Capital News* (Jefferson City, MO), May 19, 1931.
582. *Jefferson City (MO) Post-Tribune*, May 18, 1931.
583. *Daily Capital News* (Jefferson City, MO), May 19, 1931.
584. Brooks, "Open Field."
585. *Jefferson City (MO) Post-Tribune*, May 13, 1931.
586. *Jefferson City (MO) Post-Tribune*, June 20, 1932.
587. *Jefferson City (MO) Post-Tribune*, June 27, 1932.
588. *Jefferson City (MO) Post-Tribune*, July 19, 1932.
589. *Jefferson City (MO) Post-Tribune*, July 26, 1932.
590. *Jefferson City (MO) Post-Tribune*, August 23, 1932.
591. *Jefferson City (MO) Post-Tribune*, May 12, 1936.
592. *Jefferson City (MO) Post-Tribune*, May 25, 1936.
593. *Sunday News and Tribune* (Jefferson City, MO), May 17, 1936.
594. Michelle Brooks, "Local Ball Team Advanced to National Baseball Tourney," Cole County History series, *Jefferson City (MO) News Tribune*, November 1, 2020.
595. Ibid.
596. Ibid.
597. Ibid.
598. Ibid.
599. Ibid.
600. Ibid.
601. Ibid.
602. Ibid.
603. Brooks, "Open Field."
604. Ibid.

Chapter 20

605. Young, *Pioneers of High, Water and Main*.
606. *Sunday News and Tribune* (Jefferson City, MO), February 17, 1935.
607. Young, *Pioneers of High, Water and Main*.
608. *Sunday News and Tribune* (Jefferson City, MO), February 17, 1935.
609. Ibid.
610. Ibid.
611. Ibid.
612. Ibid.
613. Ibid.

614. *Kansas City (MO) Times*, January 31, 1899.
615. *History of Cole.*
616. *Daily Capital News* (Jefferson City, MO), July 27, 1923.
617. Ibid.
618. M.L. Van Nada, *The Book of Missourian: The Achievements and Personnel of Notable Living Men and Women of Missouri in the Opening Decade of the Twentieth Century* (St. Louis: T.J. Steele, 1906).
619. *History of Cole.*
620. *Daily Capital News* (Jefferson City, MO), July 27, 1923.
621. Ibid.

Chapter 21

622. Jefferson City, Missouri, Sanborn Map Company, 1898.
623. Johnston, *Illustrated Sketch Book and Directory.*
624. Ibid.
625. Ford, *History of Jefferson City.*

Chapter 22

626. Jenny Smith, unpublished notes, 2021.
627. Ibid.
628. Chris Koenig (2008) and Camilla Deiber (2015), "Missouri State Penitentiary Historic District," National Register of Historic Places, 2015.
629. Michelle Brooks, "90 Years of Shoes," Landmarks series, *Jefferson City (MO) News-Tribune*, October 18, 2015.
630. Smith, unpublished notes.
631. Ibid.
632. Ibid.
633. Johnston, *Illustrated Sketch Book and Directory.*
634. Smith, unpublished notes.
635. Johnston, *Illustrated Sketch Book and Directory.*
636. Urbana Group, "Jefferson City Historic East Architectural/Historic Survey," 1992.
637. *Daily Capital News* (Jefferson City, MO), June 30, 1943.
638. Smith, unpublished notes.

639. *Sunday News and Tribune* (Jefferson City, MO), April 14, 1947.

640. Johnston, *Illustrated Sketch Book and Directory*.

641. Smith, unpublished notes.

642. Ibid.

643. *Jefferson City (MO) Post Tribune*, April 2, 1930.

Chapter 23

644. Johnston, *Illustrated Sketch Book and Directory*.

645. Ibid.

646. Ibid.

647. *St. Louis (MO) Republic*, September 18, 1902; Hoye's Jefferson City, MO, City Directory, 1904.

648. *Daily Capital News* (Jefferson City, MO), September 3, 1922.

649. *Jefferson City (MO) Post Tribune*, January 12, 1929.

650. "Jefferson Theatre," Cinema Treasures, cinematreasures.org/theaters/12291.

651. *Daily Capital News* (Jefferson City, MO), October 24, 1924.

652. *Jefferson City (MO) Post Tribune*. April 8, 1929.

653. "Jefferson Theatre."

654. "Jefferson Theatre"; Wayne Johnson, Cole County History series, *Jefferson City (MO) News Tribune*, September 26, 2020.

655. *Sunday News and Tribune* (Jefferson City, MO), December 23, 1956.

656. *Sunday News and Tribune* (Jefferson City, MO), October 4, 1959.

657. *Daily Capital News* (Jefferson City, MO), October 14, 1969.

Chapter 24

658. "Biographical Sketch of Union Soldiers," Cole County (MO) Historical Society.

659. Johnston, *Illustrated Sketch Book and Directory*.

660. "Biographical Sketch of Union Soldiers."

661. Ibid.

662. Ibid.

663. *State Journal* (Jefferson City, MO), August 8, 1873.

664. *State Republican* (Jefferson City, MO), August 24, 1893.

665. *State Journal* (Jefferson City, MO), October 19, 1877.

666. Biographies, Cole County (MO) Historical Society.

667. Ibid.

668. Johnston, *Illustrated Sketch Book and Directory*.

669. Ibid.

670. Frank Brown Elston, "Frank Brown Elston Memoir," Ancestry.com, 2001.

Chapter 25

671. "New Buildings," *State Journal* (Jefferson City, MO), January 4, 1878; Ruthie Caplinger, "Johann Fredrick and Margaret Knaup: Jefferson City Pioneers," Cole County History series, *Jefferson City (MO) News Tribune*, October 25, 2019.

672. "New Buildings."

673. Ibid.

674. Ibid.

675. Ibid.; *State Journal* (Jefferson City, MO), September 14, 1877.

676. Caplinger, "Johann Fredrick and Margaret Knaup."

677. "Remodeling Jobs Total Over $8,000," *Sunday News and Tribune* (Jefferson City, MO), January 17, 1937.

678. Caplinger, "Johann Fredrick and Margaret Knaup."

679. Walter A. Schroeder, "The Knaup House, 400 East Capitol," *Munichburg Memories*, May 2019.

680. Ibid.

681. Caplinger, "Johann Fredrick and Margaret Knaup."

682. *People's Tribune* (Jefferson City, MO), July 10, 1878.

683. Schroeder, "The Knaup House."

684. Ibid.; Caplinger, "Johann Fredrick and Margaret Knaup."

685. Caplinger, "Johann Fredrick and Margaret Knaup."

686. Schroeder, "The Knaup House."

687. Michelle Brooks, unpublished City Hotel history, 2020.

688. *Missouri State Times*, June 30, 1865.

689. "The City Hotel," *State Journal* (Jefferson City, MO), July 12, 1878.

690. Ibid.

691. Ibid.

692. *State Republican* (Jefferson City, MO), December 22, 1892.

693. Henry Genske, email to the author, 2020.

Chapter 26

694. Smith, unpublished notes.
695. Johnston, *Illustrated Sketch Book and Directory*, 334.
696. Ibid.; *State Republican* (Jefferson City, MO), April 2, 1896.
697. Johnston, *Illustrated Sketch Book and Directory*. 334.
698. Ibid.
699. Ibid.; *Missouri Sharp Shooter*, February 26, 1904.
700. *The Southwest Mail* (Nevada, MO), February 19, 1904.

Chapter 27

701. Debbie Goldammer, unpublished notes, 2021.
702. Ibid.
703. Cole County, MO, U.S. Census, 1870; Missouri State Census, 1873.
704. *Jefferson City (MO) Daily Capital News*, September 4, 1940.
705. U.S. Register of Civil, Military and Naval Service, 1891; U.S. Appointments of U.S. Postmasters, 1832–1971.
706. *Jefferson City (MO) News and Tribune*, November 18, 1934.
707. *Daily Capital News* (Jefferson City, MO), August 28, 1917; *Jefferson City (MO) Daily Capital News*, November 13, 1919.
708. *Jefferson City (MO) Daily Capital News*, November 15, 1922.
709. *Jefferson City (MO) Daily Capital News*, January 28, 1933.
710. *Jefferson City (MO) Daily Capital News*, September 4, 1940.
711. Johnston, *Illustrated Sketch Book and Directory*.
712. Ibid.

Chapter 28

713. Goldammer, unpublished notes; Johnston, *Illustrated Sketch Book and Directory*; *St. Louis (MO) Post-Dispatch*, August 4, 1895.
714. *St. Louis (MO) Post-Dispatch*, August 4, 1895.
715. Johnston, *Illustrated Sketch Book and Directory*.
716. *St. Louis (MO) Post-Dispatch*, July 8, 1882, and August 4, 1895.
717. *St. Louis (MO) Post-Dispatch*, July 8, 1882.
718. Ibid.

719. *Jefferson City (MO) Post-Tribune*, November 16, 1917; *Daily Journal of Commerce* (Kansas City, MO), April 19, 1877.

720. *St. Louis (MO) Post-Dispatch*, July 8, 1882.

721. *St. Louis (MO) Post-Dispatch*, August 4, 1895; *St. Joseph (MO) Gazette-Herald*, August 4, 1883.

722. "Death of Henry Ewing," undated clipping.

723. *Sedalia (MO) Democrat*, July 6, 1896.

724. "Eugene Field Was First Editor Here," *University Missourian* (Columbia, MO), September 14, 1908.

725. *St. Louis (MO) Post-Dispatch*, August 4, 1895.

726. *Crawford Mirror* (Steelville, MO), December 2, 1880.

727. Goldammer, unpublished notes.

728. *St. Joseph (MO) Gazette*, July 16, 1936.

729. "Former House Veteran Dead," undated clipping.

730. Ibid.

731. "Shackleford Is Dead," *Jefferson City (MO) Post-Tribune*, July 16, 1936.

732. Ibid.

733. Jeff Davis, "The First Congressional Hearing on Highway Aid," *Transportation Weekly*, January 21, 2013, https://www.enotrans.org.

734. "The National Old Trails Road," Section 4, On Capitol Hill, https://highways.dot.gov.

735. "Shackleford Is Dead."

736. Goldammer, unpublished notes.

737. Ibid.

738. Ibid.

739. "Civil Leaders Pay Eloquent Tribute to Charles Tweedie," *Sunday News and Tribune* (Jefferson City, MO), June 17, 1945.

740. Ibid.

741. Goldammer, unpublished notes.

INDEX

ABOUT THE AUTHOR

ost Jefferson City is Michelle Brooks' third book. Her first with The History Press, *Hidden History of Jefferson City*, was released in July 2021.

Brooks' first self-published book, *Interesting Women of the Capital City*, was released in June 2021, with part of the proceeds going to support the local Zonta Club's Second Chance Scholarship.

Brooks graduated from Lincoln University in 2018 with a Bachelor of Liberal Studies degree, emphasis in anthropology and history. She is a research analyst at the Missouri State Archives. Previously, she spent twenty-five years writing for Missouri newspapers, beginning in high school, and holds many awards for her writing and her support of community organizations.

When not writing or researching, she enjoys her home and family: Stephen, William, Madison, Monroe, Tiger, Bucky, D.C. and Chester.